WILDLING

WILDLING

MY AUTOBIOGRAPHY

MICHAEL
MCINDOE

*To the one person who has stood by me
during many turbulent times.*

*You've supported me when I needed it the most.
You deserve all the praise and love I have to give.
I couldn't have written this book without you.*

*I don't say it often enough, but thank
you so much for everything.*

*You are perfect in every way and
I love you more than anything else in this entire world.*

Contents

Contents

Part III - Chinese Whispers

Acknowledgments

I would like to give thanks to the following people who have all helped and inspired me in some way. I will be forever grateful.

Mum, the McLeod family, the McCulloch family, Jimmy Elder, John Moore, Ron Jukes, Rob Watkins, Clive Gibbs, Paul Merson, Marchwood Priory, Graham Turner, ES Life Coaching, Peter and Carol Hill, the Golder family, Gary Johnson, Mark Lader, John Ryan, the Stirling family, Matthew Upson and Scott Yardley.

Michael McIndoe 2017

Part I

Caught in the Web

1
Humble Beginnings

I was born on 2nd December 1979 at the Simpson Memorial Hospital, Edinburgh to Robert and Carol McIndoe. My parents didn't stay married very long. In fact I don't ever remember them being together. My mum is a 5ft-tall Catholic with a jet-black bob; my father, a 6ft-5in ginger Protestant who, ironically, resembles Gerry Adams on steroids. He had four kids with three different women. I didn't even know about one of my brothers until I was 15. We weren't exactly a close-knit family. We saw Dad as little as possible – sometimes every two weeks, sometimes once a month. He was an aggressive man and, like a true Scotsman, very much enjoyed a drink.

When we did see him, he would drive into the estate in his brown Renault 19 to pick us up. I never really saw eye to eye with him, but the one thing we did agree on was Hearts FC. Like me, he was a massive fan and after splitting up with Mum, he moved to Gorgie Road into a tiny one-bedroom flat that backed onto Tynecastle Stadium overlooking the pitch, giving us a great view of home matches.

Mum brought up my older brother Martin and me, pretty much single-handedly. She did the best she could but I use the term 'brought up' loosely. By the time I hit my early teens I was supporting myself, making my own money through different means. I was constantly in and out of trouble, causing her a lot of problems. Mum tried her hardest but I was uncontrollable. Her time with Dad had taken its toll and their relationship had mentally scarred her.

The three of us lived together in Sighthill, on the notorious Calders housing estate, which is on the far west edge of Edinburgh. It was probably one of the most feared estates in the capital. Split into three concrete, high-rise blocks, Cobbinshaw House, Dunsyre House and Medwin House, where the three of us lived in a cramped, dated two-bedroom flat on the 11th floor. Bordering the three high-rises were lots of smaller blocks of flats. Even now, not many estates can match how tough the Calders was in the 80s and 90s. There have been numerous murders, serious assaults and stabbings over the years. The area has always had one of the highest crime rates in Edinburgh.

Most people hardly ever left the estate. It was like a confinement. It had its own shops in the centre where most of the activity took place. If you needed something this was usually a good place to start. The shops were surrounded by the high-rises, so the people living there had a bird's-eye view of whatever was going on below. If you weren't a recognised face and you were on your way to the shops, you might as well draw a big 'Fuck off' red target on your back because it was highly possible that you'd be robbed.

The majority of kids from the estate went to both

the nursery school and Sighthill Primary School. The community was tight and it was rare that any outsiders who lived off the estate would go to the school. This meant that everybody knew everybody. The school gates were about 30 metres from my block, Medwin House. My most vivid memory from my primary school days is the school-lunch queuing system. We were split into two queues, determined by income – those who could afford to pay for school lunches and those who couldn't, relying on a ticket funded by the school. I stood in the very long, latter queue and I hated it. In a place that was already tough to grow up in, the sense of inferiority I felt handing over my free meal ticket, as a kid living on a single-parent income, gnawed away at my insides. Although grateful for the free meal, I believe other kids on the estate also hated the divide that was created amongst our peers. Being the type of personality that had too much pride, I started to sell my ticket at a cut-price rate. Even though I would get less food each day, I did it just so that I wouldn't have to stand in that queue any more.

In those days the estate was mainly full of Scottish people. It was uncommon to see any foreigners. I remember an Asian family who moved onto the estate. The next day their car was petrol bombed. The day after that, petrol was poured through their letterbox and their house was set alight. Luckily no one was injured but they were moved elsewhere for their own safety. People on the estate didn't fuck about.

Poverty and deprivation were just some of the problems that were faced every day. Unemployment figures were high, with most people struggling to even maintain their benefits. A lot of families were dysfunctional or broken, leaving it up to single mums to try to instill some kind of discipline. Having very few father figures, kids ran wild without a curfew or any kind of structure. Celebrations like birthdays or Christmases were non-existent. Holidays were the stuff of dreams. Many thought you needed a passport to get out of the estate, let alone to go abroad. We barely had money for the basic essentials, so in those circumstances selling drugs became the most attractive option.

The drug trade on the estate was fiercely controlled through a hierarchy. Getting your hands on drugs was as easy as buying a pint of milk because the three high-rises were, in short, big organised drug dens. If a light was on in certain windows, it meant they were open for business. I remember seven-year-old twins selling drugs on the corner of Dunsyre. Even at that age, they were extremely clued-up on pricing and weight.

Kids were drinking and taking drugs by the age of ten. And I was no different. Substance misuse was a prominent part of everyday life, and also the major cause of the high death rate. Running down the stairs on my way to play footie, I'd have to stop and carefully step over the junkies jacking up in the corners of piss-stinking stairwells. It's not exactly the kind of thing you expect a young nipper to see, but this was the harsh reality of life. Looking back on it now, I probably should have been scared or intimidated by what I saw but for me it was normal.

2
Blade Merchant

Being raised in these conditions meant that youths were angry, desperate and desensitised to violence. Many were blade merchants and grew up forced to overanalyse anyone who walked towards them. To get around the estate you usually had to walk underneath the high-rises where there were numerous dark areas perfect for being ambushed. Thank God guns weren't as readily available in those days. They were too expensive; whereas getting hold of a knife was easy. You couldn't live on the estate and not be handy with a blade.

Gang culture was a huge part of life. Street gangs were rife throughout Edinburgh, particularly on the outskirts in the poorer areas. In the 60s and 70s a lot of large, well-known gangs existed throughout the capital, like the BarOx, the Leith Team, YBT (Young Broomhouse Team), and TCR (Tollcross Rebels) which one of my uncles ran with. Moving into the 80s many of these gangs merged together to form part of the football casuals – Hearts' Gorgie Aggro or Hibs' CCS. In the late 80s the Calders and its neighbouring rival estates, Broomhouse, Westburn and Wester Hailes, had regular, violent territorial clashes. In the early 90s I became part of the infamous Calder Youth. Day-to-day I would hang about with five other lads, but we also formed part of a much larger gang of 60 or so within the estate.

Together, me, Stevo, Tam, Chaz, Archie and Wee Shorty made a name for ourselves. We were a bunch of dangerous, unpredictable 12-13 year-olds. Many people don't realise that it's actually teenagers who commit some of the most violent acts because they feel they have something to prove. I'm not proud of a lot of the things we did then, and the others shouldn't be either. Back then we were kids with no fear, no limits and no conscience. We had very little to lose and we were tight; we spent most of our time together. We had each other's backs no matter what, and my youth with them was a fucked-up time where violence was a daily occurrence.

One particular night we were expecting trouble. We had lookouts covering the estate. About 15 of us were hanging about outside the shops, getting tooled up, when we heard that some Westburn boys had been spotted. We got as many lads together as we could and headed over to the clearing that separated the two estates. Each gang, carrying knives, bats and golf clubs, stood facing each other. I remember the overriding sense of hostility in the air. One of the older boys broke ranks and charged, with the ferocity of a caged animal breaking loose, into the other side, swinging a bat.

These fights always felt like they went on for hours. I saw kids emerging severely battered and bloodied with cracked skulls. I've got a bald patch on the back of my head where some little radgie twatted me with a crowbar.

I suppose it wasn't too dissimilar to a medieval battle: a meet on open ground, two sides waging war until one retreats and waves the white flag. The ones who caused the most damage or the most serious injuries were hailed as heroes.

It wasn't just rival estates that felt the brutality of the Calder Youth; we hated the police too. They weren't welcome on the estate and that seemed to be the general attitude. In fact people had even tried to burn down Wester Hailes police station. We policed ourselves and protected our own. The police sometimes turned up in their meat wagons, heavy-handed, wearing riot gear to arrest people. I remember a time when they tried to edge forwards through the estate but were met with bricks and bottles. More people joined the commotion, screaming at them to fuck off, attacking from all angles. The situation escalated. They'd positioned themselves like sitting ducks and soon there was a full-blown riot. I could hear my mum screaming at me from the flat window to get my arse back home. I was only about 12 years old. I ignored her and stood my ground with the others. The police were funnelled in and things turned nastier. Glass Irn-Bru bottles were used as petrol bombs. Those who couldn't get the technique right dropped the glass bottle and watched it blow up in front of them, which isn't ideal when you're busting a nylon shell suit. Unable to contain the violence, the police were forced to retreat.

There were many occasions where the entire estate would group together to cause havoc, provoked or not.

After all, there was little else to do other than get high, get wasted or incite violence. But more often than not, the six of us managed to get up to no good all on our own.

There was a kid called Eddie who used to buy drugs off us now and then. He must have been a year or so older than us and he was a tall, gangly thing. He wasn't the brightest spark, which made him an easy target. Some of the lads were cruel to him and used him for their warped enjoyment. Chaz had a nasty streak and got a lot of amusement out of inflicting pain on others; he definitely had a screw loose. So when Eddie showed up, he began taunting him. Archie grabbed Eddie's arm and held it tight while pinning the rest of his body to the wall. Then Chaz held a lighter to Eddie's arm. I could see his skin blistering from the heat of the flame. Eddie frantically tried to pull away. I was rolling a joint but Eddie's screaming was putting me off. These kinds of malicious acts never sat well with me. I told Chaz to give it a rest and they let him go. Eddie made sure he grabbed his gear, though, before running off. I don't think he ever came to see us again.

3
Hampden Roar

Despite being little fuckers, we played a lot of football. I'd been playing for the primary school team which had some talented players. The pitch was smaller than a standard one, but our centre-half player, Big Toe, would score from goal kicks using the best toe bash I've ever seen. To strengthen his legs, his old man used to strap weights to his ankles and make him run.

Many of the kids were fit and very quick. You had to be fast if you wanted to dodge the police. We played out until the early hours of the morning, and it was here that I really started to learn my football skills. There would always be a big group of us kicking the ball against the shops' metal shutters. When the ball hit the steel, I used to pretend the sound was the crowd roaring at Hampden Park.

During those days we would come up with all sorts of games to test our ability. Boys will be boys, but because of our harsh upbringing, our way of thinking led us to create some pretty aggressive games. Most of the games involved hurting each other. I remember playing a particularly vicious game called 'Five and a kick up the arse'. If you missed the goal you'd become goalkeeper. If you conceded five goals, everybody playing got to kick you up the arse as hard as they could. There could be 10 to 20 kids playing at any time, and each one would put all their effort into making sure you were black and blue. You stood, clenching your butt and cupping your bollocks, praying that no one would clip them when they put the boot in. The more goals you let in, the more kicks you received. There were many nights when I was barely able to walk home. But playing this for hours on end taught me a valuable lesson – make sure you hit the target.

I stayed out all day and all night getting high, causing trouble and playing football. We didn't care what the time was. I never wanted to be indoors because there was nothing to do and very little food in the fridge. We did have a rented TV – with a money box on the back which you had to put coins in. It was like a pay-as-you-go system so it didn't work if you had no money. I remember how pissed off I used to get when the TV credit ran out halfway through a film. Now and again I'd kick open the money box on the back of the TV so I could buy food. On the odd occasion I was at home, I slept in a windowless box room. Dad had built a coffin-like bed, a foot from the ceiling with a desk and clothes rail underneath. When the bedroom door opened, it left me just enough room to slide in sideways before it hit the side of the bed. I hated it so much that sometimes I would climb into the lift shaft and sit on top of the lift in my building. I could smoke there in peace and I enjoyed listening to people's conversations when they got into the lift.

As I grew older my love of football didn't diminish. As

well as playing for the Sighthill Primary team, I played for Salvesen boys club, then moved to Hutchinson Vale boys club. During this time I started my short-lived secondary education at Tynecastle High School.

After a couple of seasons at Hutchinson Vale, through one of my dad's friends, I switched clubs to Musselburgh Union. I remember enjoying it there a hell of a lot more than any of my previous clubs, even though the team was on the opposite side of Edinburgh. Mum didn't have a car so I had to take two long bus rides to training twice a week. I'd be drained by the time I got there and it'd be at least midnight by the time I got home, but I didn't care, I just wanted to play. I really enjoyed the competitive side of football, meeting new people and discovering life off the estate. Sometimes I'd arrive at training with no idea how I'd get home because I didn't have enough money for the return journey. For those times I will always be thankful to Ryan Hush and his dad, who'd give me a lift back to the edge of the Calders in their bottle-green Jag. I have fond memories of us singing to 'Wonderwall' by Oasis on the journey home.

I got a lucky break in my early teens when I was asked to play for Hibs FC, alongside my Hutchinson Vale teammate Kenny Miller. This was my first professional club at schoolboy level. The only problem was, I lived and breathed Hearts FC. My family are Hearts fans, and I come from an area on the west side where almost everybody is a diehard Hearts fan – the exception being the McCleod family, who were fully fledged Hibs fans. No other fucker

I knew had had this opportunity, but I knew my loyalty would always lie with Hearts. It's my club and that will never change. So the day I put on that Hibs shirt was an odd one, with very mixed emotions.

4
The Drug Debt

By now I was travelling to and from Tynecastle High School every day and I was going to Musselburgh twice a week. Despite any talent I had for the game, I was torn between drugs, violent gang culture and football. I was selling more, so I naturally started taking more.

At first I don't think anyone noticed. I was still performing well but the more I became embroiled in my self-destructive path, the more football took a back seat. I missed a lot of training, including trials for Chelsea and Scotland. I remember one of the Musselburgh Union coaches, Scott Robertson, making journeys up to the estate to speak to Mum to try to find out what was going on. The drugs, as they do, had caused a change in my personality; I'd become more aggressive. I'm grateful now for the help Scott tried to give me, but it didn't make a difference because at that time nobody could tell me what to do. I lived a very independent life. Sometimes I wouldn't come home for days on end. There were no mobiles in those days so Mum would only see me when I decided to show my face. Over the years she became hardened and accustomed to the fact that I was out doing my own thing.

I looked up to drug dealers and underworld figures who seemed so successful, always wearing the latest designer clothes and driving what we thought were flash cars. There were no other mentors to teach me anything different. There was a youth centre on the estate for a while, and my mum did some work there. But it had so many unpredictable, temperamental kids who were high on drug cocktails that they shut it down.

In my own drug-fuelled brain, I didn't believe that playing football was ever going to be a real option for me. So I carried on taking more and more drugs, allowing myself to be spun ever tighter in an already entangled web. The gang got into fights regularly. Whether they were for a just cause or not, it didn't matter; it was the done thing.

We were all trying to escape the cold one night by standing in the chippy, when a man came in we didn't know. Tam piped up and told him to buy us a bag of chips. He said no, so Stevo punched him in the face, which floored him. I remember the owner slipping off to avoid getting caught in the crossfire as Tam and Wee Shorty started laying into him, stamping on his head. The man's face was covered in blood. I grabbed Tam and Wee Shorty and pulled them away, pushing them out of the door. Stevo had started it for no reason, and deep down I knew he had a really sinister side to him. It wasn't right. I mean, what a fucking liberty. The poor guy had done nothing wrong, but this event summed up the mindset and volatility of the estate.

I tried to steer the lads away from this kind of bullshit. In my view we'd made a name for ourselves already, so picking on innocent bystanders was pointless. By 13, I'd grown up way beyond my years. I'd seen things no child should ever see. In fact most people will never see in an entire lifetime the amount of violence I'd been exposed to. Of course I did stupid things I regret now; I wouldn't be human if I didn't. But it was the only life I knew. From my parents, to my friends, to other people on the estate, it was the same story; the only behaviour I ever witnessed or understood was filled with anger and violence. I didn't have the privilege of living in an environment filled with love and laughter.

After a year or so, I didn't bother with high school that much. My loyalty was to the boys. School didn't engage me and I couldn't get my head around it. I'd been asked a few times by the football coach, Mr Highland, to play for the school football team, but even that didn't tempt me. We were busy selling drugs and trying to make money. It was going well for a while, until Chaz ran up a drug debt with Crazy Rab, one of the older lot. As a group, we'd agreed to take on a certain amount, but the dumb fucker had been talked into taking on four times more – yet he'd still agreed to pay it back within the usual time period. The money had to be paid within two weeks, and selling all the drugs in that time was going to be a mammoth task. We decided the best course of action was to head off alone and sell on other estates. Choosing to do this was risky but it was the only choice we had.

I decided to go to Broomhouse as I knew its layout quite well. I waited by the shops. In the first couple of hours I shifted a bit, but it was going to take all day and all night to sell what I had on me. I knew I was on borrowed time; it was a blatant piss-take just being there, let alone boldly selling on another estate. A fat kid approached, who looked a few years older than me, and indicated that he wanted to do a deal. He said he wasn't comfortable doing it in the open and so I should follow him around the back of the shops. Alarm bells were ringing in my head but I needed the sale so I went with him.

We stopped by a car that had two lads leaning against it. Instinct told me that this kid and the two lads were together. It was highly possible that they were part of the next-generation YBT gang. I had the shop wall behind me, the lads to my right and the fat kid to my left. I felt like I was penned in. The kid reached into his jacket to get what I thought was his money, but instead he pulled out a fucking axe. My natural reaction kicked in and I flicked out my blade to protect myself. The mad fat bastard swung the axe wildly. I ducked just in time, narrowly avoiding it ramming into the side of my head. My instincts had been right. The other two lads, one of whom was holding some kind of cosh, had now joined him, and they were blocking my way out. My heart pounded in my chest. He swung the axe again. I dodged again but felt a blow to my ribs from the lad with the cosh. The blade I had was small and I knew I had to get out of there; otherwise I was going to get fucked up. I jumped over the car bonnet and sprinted as fast as I could up the Calder Road straight back to my estate.

The other lads had managed to sell some bits, but

nowhere near enough to cover the debt. Over the next few days we were out and about selling as much as we could. By the following Wednesday we were still unable to cover the full amount. With 48 hours until the deadline, Chaz had come back in a panic because he'd been gripped up by Crazy Rab, who'd heard we were struggling to get rid of it. He held a crossbow to Chaz's head, warning him in no uncertain terms that he'd settle for nothing less than the full amount. If we didn't pay up he'd put a hole in Chaz – and it wasn't an empty threat.

Even at the age of 14 we could each hold our own, but Crazy Rab was part of the older gang on the estate and there were certain people you just didn't fuck with. He was a twisted motherfucker who would get a lot of enjoyment out of hurting Chaz. The message was crystal clear.

The following day, somehow, Crazy Rab got his money in full. I knew better than to ask any questions so I just went with the flow. That weekend we had a party. It was a heavy couple of days. The next thing I knew I was being shaken awake in the early hours of the morning by a face I didn't recognise. He was shouting at me to get my fucking arse up. I had no idea who he was or what was going on. As I sat up, groggy and out of it, I saw a few men in suits and heard someone say, "Police, CID."

My head was banging. Then I heard someone say I was to be questioned about an armed robbery. I could hear some of the gang being rounded up in the next room. I was dragged into an unmarked blue Ford Fiesta and taken to the station. Being questioned by the police wasn't a new experience for any of us. I was a minor so they contacted Mum, but I wasn't worried because I didn't know anything about it. Later that morning I was released without any charge.

5
Meeting the Devil

1993 was my introduction to the rave scene. Thousands of people from all over would descend on Ingliston in Edinburgh for 'Rezerection'. This rave lasted all night and attracted some big names like Carl Cox, N-Joi and Ratpack. The drug of choice was ecstasy, so there was very little trouble at these events due to the shared feeling of euphoria. It was a nice reprieve from the constant fighting.

A stupid mindset prevailed on the estate; we wanted to see who could pop the most pills. Teenagers would up the ante, insisting on playing Russian roulette with other dangerous drugs like methadone. Despite being a prescription-only drug, administered to junkies who are trying to wean themselves off heroin, they would consume just a little of their prescribed medication and sell the rest on. Methadone overdoses, sadly, took the lives of too many teenagers on the estate, some of whom were good friends of mine.

I came close myself; an LSD overdose nearly killed me. One day I found myself 11 floors up, the window wide open, thinking I had the ability to fly. The environment you are in hugely affects your state of mind. And anyone who has taken hallucinogenic drugs will know how this substance plays tricks on your brain. I truly believed I could fly. Half hanging out the window, Mum grabbed me just in time but she wasn't strong enough to stop me from climbing out. I was fixated on trying to get out of that window. If my older brother Martin hadn't been there, I would definitely have died that day. He and Mum's boyfriend dragged me back in and locked me in my little windowless bedroom.

As the door shut, I found myself in an uncontrollable state of panic and fear. Screaming hysterically, I frantically tried to get out of the room. I had completely lost my mind. I started to see monsters attacking me. I couldn't see a way out. I couldn't escape. I felt claustrophobic. The walls started to close in on me. I couldn't breathe. Using my arms and legs, I tried desperately to push the walls back. My hands were so sweaty they kept slipping as I tried to stop the walls from squashing me. No matter how loud I shouted or how much I cried, no one opened the door. My brain couldn't handle the things I was seeing and I felt like my head was going to explode. When a dark hooded figure appeared by the side of my bed, I knew it was the devil himself. He just hovered next to me. Staring. I thought I was going to die alone and terrified, shut in that little room I hated so much. Drenched in sweat I closed my eyes, waiting for the darkness to come, believing that this was my end. But then I heard his voice say that next time he would take me with him.

My ordeal lasted nearly 14 hours. When I finally came to my senses I started to question what the fuck I was doing with my life. I'd petrified Mum, and my brother was furious. I knew I'd had a lucky escape and from that day on, I made a conscious decision to never ever touch drugs again. Even from a young age, once I put my mind to something I'd stick to it, but being around the gang was difficult now. I could finally see everything for the ego trip it was. Maybe I was maturing? Maybe my brain was clearing from the drugs it had been so used to? One thing I was sure about, though, was how guilty I felt about the things we had done. When one of the boys went to attack an innocent bystander with a claw hammer, I jumped on him before he could swing. I seemed to be growing a conscience. I was beginning to wonder what I was even doing in the gang. But what happened next would take me away from that life forever.

My uncle always had his ear close to the ground. He'd heard a rumour that one of us was going to get seriously hurt, and something about us having been causing too much trouble. I took in what he was saying but didn't really think too much about it over the coming weeks.

Late one night I returned from a football training session and, as usual, walked from the bus stop on the main road into the estate. Arriving at Medwin House, I jumped into the lift and then knocked on my flat door. Mum opened it looking traumatised. She told me Stevo had been stabbed and was in a really bad way. I threw my football boots to the floor and sprinted down the stairs to look for the boys. Chaz's place was the closest so I started my search there. I hammered on the front door and Chaz let me in. The rest of the gang were already there. I sat down and Tam filled me in on what had happened.

A kid, formerly from Wester Hailes, who had recently moved into the Calders, had come looking for a fight. A few of the lads were outside the chemist. The boys said they'd started laughing at this kid because he was jumping up and down, giving it. Stevo decided to give him what he'd come for. Fighting was a normal occurrence outside the shops so everyone just let them get on with it. They stepped up to each other and started throwing punches. Stevo quickly got the kid in a headlock but within a split second the lad had pulled out a long knife and sliced Stevo's stomach clean open. Not realising he was wounded, Stevo continued fighting for a few seconds, but as the colour drained from his face he collapsed to the floor. His insides were hanging out of his open stomach. Chaz's dad Frank, who had been on his way to buy fags, saw the commotion and ran over to help. He had military experience from the Falklands and reacted quickly. He somehow managed to scoop Stevo's insides back in and put pressure on the huge wound until the ambulance turned up. In the meantime Matty, one of the older lads, jumped on top of the kid and battered the fuck out of him. He was barely moving by the end of his mauling. The estate may have been many things but it didn't breed grasses and even though this kid had ripped open one of our own, I was told the knife was disposed of.

Stevo lost a lot of blood and had to undergo emergency surgery. Frank had played a huge part in saving his life that night. Stevo was released from hospital a couple of weeks later with 52 stitches across his abdomen. This was the first time that one of our own gang had been close to death due to violence. Sure we'd had injuries from beatings and other minor slashings, but nothing like this. In the days after the incident I couldn't help but remember the warning my uncle had given me, which I'd casually dismissed. It could have been any one of us that night.

The streets were no longer enjoyable and as I wasn't taking drugs any more, I was seeing life through different eyes. It was a surreal experience. I'd missed a lot of football training in the last few months, but that night, to keep out of trouble, I'd decided to start going again. I'll always wonder, if I hadn't gone to training, would it have been me? After that, I thanked God every day for a long time. It was a real turning point for me, and the first time I'd ever really considered what life might be like outside the gang.

6
Changing Direction

Shortly after Stevo's attack, my dad picked me up and we drove over to Gorgie Road. When we got to his place I made myself at home on the sofa and turned on the TV. Suddenly Dad turned on me and grabbed my leg with his giant hands. He dragged my leg onto the pine coffee table in front of me and pushed his foot down onto my knee. I winced in pain. He looked me in the eyes and growled in his deep Scottish accent that I needed to make a decision – football or the gang. He threatened to break my leg if I chose the gang. I could tell by his tone that he wasn't bluffing.

Some might think that's a bit harsh, some may disagree, but where I come from, if you don't fear it, you don't respect it. My dad was a huge man with a temper to match. Trust me when I say you never wanted to be on the receiving end of a slap or a punch from him because his hands were enormous. I was always very careful around him, as you never knew when his unpredictable temper would make him explode and lash out.

I had no doubt in my head that Dad would have put his size 12s through my kneecap. I knew what he was trying to do but I'd already started to consider the path I wanted to take; I'd stopped taking drugs, and the things I'd seen more recently had made me stop and think about the gang and its choices anyway. It took me all of about a second to reply. Obviously I chose football.

Dad stepped off the table and let me have my leg back intact. We continued the discussion calmly. He told me to go to work as a labourer with my Uncle Forbes down in the Leith Docks to earn a wage. As my older brother Martin was spending more time at my dad's, it was decided that I would do the same to keep me away from the estate. At this point I knew I was done with gang culture and its lifestyle. For the first time in my life I could see a way out.

As agreed, I started to spend more time at Gorgie Road even though I had to sleep on the floor. His one-bedroom flat was tiny. Despite his marriage failing with my mum, he went on to meet Caroline, who was always good to me and they had a son together called Sam. My dad, Caroline, Martin, Sam and I would all cram in somehow and make the best of what we had. It wasn't exactly happy families but it was the lesser of two evils. Tynecastle High School was a minute's walk away and even though I'd missed a lot of school, I did pop in from time to time. At weekends I'd meet up with school friends at the Locarno Snooker Club.

I did as my old man suggested and at the age of 15 I took a job with my Uncle Forbes. I'd arrive at his yard in Leith Docks for 7am and work from Monday to Friday. I was given all sorts of unique jobs to do, like digging 6ft by 2ft holes in the hills. I never asked any questions but the police stopped me on numerous occasions. I just told them I was working for my Uncle Forbes and shrugged my shoulders. He was a bit of a character and rumoured to be one of Scotland's best safe-blowers.

7
The Boys in Maroon

The best bit about being at Dad's was that his flat backed onto Tynecastle Stadium, the home of Hearts FC. We lived on the top floor so our three windows overlooked the away stand behind the goal, giving us an unbelievable view of the pitch. It was the best free seat in the house. Every Saturday I would get up early and clean the stairs in the block, charging £2 per flat for the service. Then I would babysit my little brother for an hour or so before heading off to play for Musselburgh Union, making sure I was back in time for the Hearts kick-off at 3pm. It was my favourite day of the week. Saturday's at the flat were always very busy with Dad's friends or my uncles all cramming into the small living room to watch the match from the window and then me, my brothers, plus our friends squeezing into the bedroom to watch from there. The atmosphere in the stadium was phenomenal. By now I was living and breathing the game. I couldn't get enough of it.

Depending on when I finished my own matches, sometimes before the Hearts game, Dad would take Martin and me down to the Green Tree pub where my Uncle Vinnie was a bouncer. He'd sneak us in the side door where we'd play pool and drink shandy. A lot of fans would be in the pub, getting in some last-minute beers before the match. I first experienced football hooliganism here. It was one of the last pubs before you reached the stadium's away entrance, so thousands of fans who'd travelled across the country would jump off the train at Haymarket and go through Dalry before marching down Gorgie Road shouting, singing and smashing shop windows. Derby days produced the most violent clashes between Hearts and Hibs supporters. The casuals ran riot, causing havoc along the road with scarves covering their faces. The pub was petrol-bombed a few times. It was always a trouble hotspot, especially during the bigger games, due to its location. But I really enjoyed the mood in the pub and how the game united everyone.

Just before kick-off we'd hurry back to the flat and settle in to watch the game. The whole of Gorgie would be engulfed in excitement. Before matches the away fans would ring the flat buzzer non-stop to offer my dad money, hoping they'd be allowed to watch the game from the flat or gain access to the roof. The only thing separating the flats from the stadium was a 30ft garden. Next to the away entrance was a wall, and whenever Hibs, Celtic or Rangers played at Tynecastle, the away fans who were unable to get tickets would climb over this wall into the flat gardens where other fans would pull them up into the stadium. At other times neighbours would leave ladders in their gardens and the fans could prop them up against the stadium wall and climb over into the stand like Apache warriors invading a fort.

It was customary for away fans, if their team was losing, to turn round and throw coins at the flat windows. They'd know which windows were Hearts supporters because they'd have flags or scarves hanging outside. Dad had several windows replaced because of angry fans smashing them. I used to run down after the match into the gardens and collect the money that had been chucked, earning me a good £5-£9 most weeks. It soon dawned on Dad that he should buy the away team's flag and hang it out of the window alongside our Hearts flag as a deterrent. This seemed to work for a while, until I had some of the lads over from Musselburgh Union to watch a midweek match, including my pal Marc McCulloch. We were watching Hearts vs Dundee United. Marc, always the joker, thought it would be funny to moony at the away fans during half-time. In a matter of seconds the window came in – shards of glass flew everywhere, all over Marc and the rest of us. Hearing the glass shattering from the other room, Dad came storming in. He looked at the mess and grabbed hold of me by the throat, lifting me off my feet. I could smell the stench of alcohol on his breath as he bellowed in my face, blaming me for the mess. Naturally I didn't grass Marc up. They knew Dad was in his usual pissed state and would put me down soon. The lads were used to him being a bit of a nutter.

***

After a few beers, Dad would bang on about Freemason history. I remember he'd studied architecture at Napier University, so despite his obvious flaws he was actually an intelligent man. It was all pretty interesting stuff but having a family with such different views on religion and seeing some of the arguments it caused over the years, I steered clear of getting involved. But I think that's why the windows were always fixed so quickly, and for free – Dad must have had some handy links through the Lodge.

***

At the away end, the stewards would open the big maroon gates during the last 15 minutes of the match. Sometimes I'd run down, hoping the stewards would be in a good mood and allow me to go through the gates into the stadium. I'd get to watch the remaining minutes up close, just so I could say I'd been. It would be rammed and the crowd swallowed me up. I'd just stand and soak up the atmosphere, waving up at the flat hoping they could see me. Later in the evening we'd always sit down to watch Sports Scene (the Scottish version of Match of the Day) to see if we'd made it on TV. The camera would scan across the crowd, now and again zooming in on the flats to film the fans at the windows.

My most vivid memory was the night when Bayern Munich came to play us in the UEFA Cup; Iain Ferguson scored an unbelievable 25-yard free kick. It was an absolute corker and the place erupted. I remember the white and maroon scarves being swung above everyone's heads and the sound of the crowd singing in unison. We won 1-0. It was an unforgettable moment.

8
The Long Trip South

I was now spending more time at football training, which was definitely a positive, and I had more structure to my life. I'd begun playing as left back, then spent some time in the old sweeper position, and then into midfield. The physical training I was enduring at Musselburgh Union was hard, and coupled with labouring with my uncle every day, I was knackered.

The season was coming to an end and quite a few players in the league had already been signed by professional clubs and were moving south of the border. A few of the lads I played with at Musselburgh, including Marc, had signed with St Johnstone. No opportunities had come up for me yet and Musselburgh didn't have an amateur side at the time, so I signed with Links United for the new season, along with my Musselburgh teammate Stuart Fraser.

Just before my 16th birthday I got a parts apprentice job in a Peugeot garage so I stopped labouring with my Uncle Forbes. I felt quite proud as it was my first shirt-and-tie job. The slight downside was that the garage was closer to the Calders. I'd kept myself out of trouble for some time, but deep down knew I could still be lured back into that gang culture so I tried to keep off the estate as much as possible. However, I'd never forget where I'd come from; I know that side of me will always be there because it's been bred into me. I'd heard that Chaz had taken a machete to the back of the head in a retaliation attack; he had needed 120 stitches. The 'old' me was angry that I hadn't been around to watch his back, but I knew I no longer had a future there. My life was going in a different direction and I wasn't sad to be leaving it all behind.

A few months into my job at Peugeot, the manager at Musselburgh Union, Jimmy Elder, invited my dad and me to a meeting at the Ravelston House Hotel in Musselburgh to have a chat. It was completely out of the blue. We met in the bar. Jimmy announced that four of us had been selected for youth team trials down at Luton Town FC.

I was so thrilled my stomach was doing somersaults. I knew it was only a trial but, until now, I genuinely thought I'd missed my chance. I'd given up any hope of playing football as a career and was just playing for fun. Jimmy had told the other boys and their families individually; we were the last to be told, so my old man got the beers in to celebrate. It turned out the Luton Town coach, John Moore, had been up in Scotland visiting his family and had come to watch his grandson play football. Afterwards he'd walked over to the next field where we were playing one of our last games of the season. At full-time he approached Jimmy and asked if Gary Simba, David Reiley, Stuart Fraser and myself could go down to Luton for a trial.

I was so happy and grateful to Jimmy for playing such a huge part in taking me to Musselburgh Union in the first place – and for putting up with me! I knew he'd stuck his neck out a few times when I probably didn't deserve it. I was well aware that I'd been a bit of a nightmare over the years. The only problem I had now was my job at Peugeot. As soon as I arrived at work the following morning, I spoke to my boss and asked if I could have some time off. I explained the situation but as I hadn't been there long, he wasn't keen. I thought he was going to say no, but the look on my face must have been so eager that he gave in and let me have the five days off I needed. I jumped on a National Express bus and made the 11-hour journey down south.

It had been prearranged that we'd stay with a family in Toddington during our five-day trial. We began on the Monday morning. The pressure I felt was nerve-wracking. I was very aware that every time I touched the ball or had a shot at the goal, I was being scrutinised and this could make or break my future.

We obviously did okay because out of the four of us, John asked Stuart and me to return for a second trial the following week. I was looking forward to going back but I knew my boss was going to be difficult. He'd reluctantly let me have time off and I was worried about asking again. When I told him Luton Town wanted me for another trial the next week, he said he'd have to sack me if I decided to go. I was torn. I'd just got my first proper job but I'd also just been given the opportunity to play football. My dream. There was no guarantee I'd even pass the second trial. Was it worth the risk? Mulling over my choices, I couldn't help but think this was my last chance. I'd already missed the Chelsea trials and Scotland trials, both because of drugs. How many more times could Jimmy stick his neck out for me? Fuck it, I knew had to go.

The following morning I told my boss I was leaving. It was a gamble but this was a once-in-a-lifetime opportunity. He understood and wished me luck. It was a shame as I'd just started to settle in and had even been playing for Peugeot's five-a-side team. I packed my bag and before I left for the morning bus, I promised Mum two things if I made it: a holiday and a house off the estate.

I jumped on the National Express bus again for the long journey. I was apprehensive but very excited. I could feel the fire burning in my stomach, and I was determined that this was going to be my last journey down. Kids like me from the Calders don't get opportunities like this. Leaving the city, I stared out of the coach window and caught a final glimpse of the high-rises on the estate.

Archie is dead. RIP.

Chaz is still living on the estate.

Stevo is serving a long prison sentence.

Tam is dead. RIP.

Wee Shorty is somewhere in the Borders.

Part II

Learning the Trade

9
The Old System

I didn't want to have any regrets at my second Luton Town trial so I went all out and hoped my best would be good enough. I ran around as much as I could, shouting for the ball and being visible, praying that I stood out.

After an intense week, the coach John Moore told me and Stuart that we'd both be offered two-year apprenticeships, giving us the chance to become professionals if we were good enough and worked hard. Feeling like I was in a dream, I signed a contract making my apprenticeship official. All those hours I'd spent on the bus travelling to training had finally paid off. I knew it was just an apprenticeship but I was one step closer to becoming a professional. I was under no illusion that this still might not work out, but as I scrawled my name on the dotted line I couldn't disguise my genuine smile.

The terms of the contract were pretty straightforward. My food and accommodation were sorted. I would be staying in digs – that is, I'd be living with another family for the season. The families are usually paid by the football club to put you up. Most of these digs are within close range of the club grounds. I had to go to college every Thursday, and I'd earn £32.50 per week for the first year, increasing to £37.50 per week for the second year.

John Moore arranged it so that different characters were put together in one dressing room. A lot of the players came from Hertfordshire or London, with many coming up from the Luton schoolboy team, but only a handful of us had travelled from other parts of the UK. I was glad to have Stuart there as a friendly face. It took time to get to know everyone and work the boys out, but I quickly realised their backgrounds were worlds away from mine.

Many of the kids were just an hour or two from home. After Saturday youth team matches their parents would pick them up to take them home, so they always enjoyed a bit of family life. However I spent seven days a week in my digs. Being so far away from anything familiar was a huge adjustment for me. I'd left everything I'd known in Scotland. It was difficult and took some time to get to grips with my new life. I'd also naïvely assumed I would just be playing football every day – and after labouring with my uncle, I figured this was going to be a breeze – but this couldn't have been further from the truth. The next two years were going to be tougher than I could ever have imagined!

Every Monday morning, John announced our jobs for the week. Each apprentice was assigned two professional footballers who they had to look after and run chores for. I was given Mitchell Thomas and Julian James. It was to teach us about responsibility and to make sure we were on top of our shit because if it wasn't right, fuck me, did they moan.

At 8:15am, I'd start my day at the football ground at

Kenilworth Road. I began by cleaning my boots and both my pros' boots. I'd clean their toilets and their baths, before laying out their fluffy towels. I'd make them a nice hot cup of tea or coffee and lay their kit out ready for them to start training. Once they left to train I'd then go to youth team training. We did three training sessions over the course of a day. The pros finished at 1pm so we'd fit their chores in around our training slots. On top of this the pros would give us extra jobs to do like cleaning their cars, putting on bets and polishing their shoes – Mitchell had a lot of shoes! Basically anything they couldn't be arsed to do themselves. Our final session would be under the away stand with John. He'd have us playing head tennis for hours, helping us to develop our touch skills and reactions.

After training we'd split up and were made to clean the grounds, scrub the toilets, mop the floors and anything else John or the coaches told us to do. Every Friday, he'd do spot checks and if work hadn't been carried out to his high standards, he'd punish the whole team by making us start all over again. Nothing could have prepared me for the amount of work we did. When I laboured with my uncle, all the tools would have to be put away properly and the place left spotless ready for the next day. I thought he was thorough until I met John.

Any footballer who has done one of the old apprenticeships will understand when I say it's hard graft. Now, I completely understand the harsh mentality behind the old system. Unfortunately it became frowned upon and was replaced with youth academies. It's a shame because you were moulded to develop good habits and to take hard work in your stride. But most importantly, I was taught that if you fail to do your best at all times or fail to keep your eye on the ball then it will have repercussions for your whole team. Nowadays the academy teams are not put through their paces like we were back then. Rather than strengthening a player's mental state and preparing them for what is to come if they turn pro – like the pressure they face when taking a penalty in front of thousands of baying fans – young players now are babied. Their kit is already laid out for them and they spend more time looking in the mirror than they do on the pitch.

Under Lennie Lawrence, John Moore, Wayne Turner and Trevor Peake, Luton Town was fantastic. They were all good at different things. Lennie was the 'laid-back, assess from afar' type; Wayne helped me a lot with my technique; and Trevor was the 'go to' if you needed a boost; but John, for me, was my mentor. He was Scottish, so we had instant common ground. He had a proven track record for identifying young talent from any background and developing them into professionals. He pinpointed your strengths and weaknesses and could make you cry or laugh in a second. John also had the ability to make you believe you were the best player in the world. As a faithful Christian, he instilled certain traits into his players and a strong mentality that very few coaches could achieve. Everyone listened to what he said and over a six-month training period with him, the lads noticeably improved.

My time at Luton was more fulfilling than anything

I'd ever done before. It was a million miles away from the former life I once knew. It was physically and mentally challenging. The best thing about my new life was how much food I could eat! The club chefs would prepare breakfast and lunch for all the lads. I'd spent much of my childhood hungry; now being in a place where I could eat regular healthy meals meant I could fill my belly to bursting point every day. A lot of the lads couldn't believe how much food I could tuck away. I looked like a skinny little thing but I had the appetite of about four grown men.

My focus was on training. I was developing quickly and I was pleased with my progress. I found the pressure of football easier to take than some of the other lads – probably because I'd experienced more intense situations in my life. I was also determined not to go back to where I came from.

John had a deep Scottish accent and he would say to us, "You need to fight harder sonny, to take a first team shirt. It's not going to be given to you because all those players have mouths to feed. The only way to take their job is to impress the manager."

A football club is like a conveyor belt. Each first team player is constantly looking over his shoulder, trying his best to hold down his position in the team. He knows that he has several other players, including the youth and reserves, gunning to take his position off him. It was the first time I'd started to see a more ruthless side to football.

Unfortunately I wasn't getting on well at the digs I was staying in; they had domestic problems and I didn't want to be around that environment. It reminded me of the shit I'd left behind. I approached the coaches to ask if they could find me a different family. The coaching staff were understanding and moved me. They put me in a place at Bury Park, which is in the centre of Luton right next to the football ground, with a little old Irish woman. The location was excellent and despite probably being the palest person the town had ever seen, I felt really at home. The culture was very diverse. It was completely new to me and I loved it.

However the woman I lived with wasn't so great. She locked pretty much every door inside the house, including the kitchen – and with the poor dog inside. She refused to wash any laundry and the food was awful, but I didn't want to kick up a fuss as I'd only just moved. So I spoke to some of the lads about it to see if anyone else had similar problems. Stuart, the lucky git, had bagged himself a really nice family with a massive house and a snooker room. The other lads also had decent digs. I decided I had to speak to the coaches again to see what they thought. I felt because she was old, she might not be able to manage the extra strain I was putting on her. The coaches were shocked and sent someone to the house to take a look. They couldn't believe they were paying her to look after me.

I was moved again for the third time in six months. I didn't have much luck with digs. Over the course of my apprenticeship I was moved five times, which is quite unusual. A lot of the families I moved to hadn't been tried or tested and I think I got a bit of a raw deal. I'm not sure many of them could understand what I was saying due to my accent, but I spent most of my time at the club anyway and I kept myself to myself when I was at my digs.

I became good friends with our centre half Matthew Upson. He was older than me but we played in the same youth team. He'd been staying with some lovely people, Peter and Carol Hill. Matt always spoke highly of them and when he got a move to Arsenal, he rang to tell me that he'd put a good word in for me and I could go and stay there. It was the first time I'd felt comfortable in digs. They really looked after me and it was probably the only time in my life that I was settled in a stable family environment, which definitely helped my football. Matt is a top bloke with one of the best left foots I've ever seen. I'll always be grateful to him for thinking of me when he left Luton. I don't think he really knew how much it helped me out.

**

Traditionally at Christmas, each first year apprentice had to sing a song. It sounds easy, but this had to be done standing on a chair, naked, wearing a piece of tinsel wrapped around your knob, and a pair of wellies stuffed with flour and eggs. The song had to be sung in front of all the professionals in the home team dressing room. The apprentices would cram into the boot room, shitting themselves, waiting to be called. If the pros thought you were crap they would throw tomatoes at you from close range. The two singers voted the worst would have to race around the pitch completely naked in front of even more people. I chose to sing my national anthem. My tactic was to make sure the song was easy to sing along to. When I got halfway through, some of the lads started to sing with me and I knew I was safe.

Matt Spring and Emmerson Boyce were voted the worst two singers that Christmas. I can't remember what they sang but they were terrible. Nerves had got to them. They raced each other around the pitch naked and the entire team cheered in the stands. Springy lost and had to face the first team in the tunnel. He was drenched with ice buckets but took it all in good humour, as it was intended.

The following year one of the apprentices pissed himself he was so nervous and embarrassed. Afterwards one of the mums came in to complain that the tradition was a form of bullying, so it was stopped. It sounds like a stupid thing to do now, but in my opinion it was just character-building. How can you perform in front of tens of thousands of people confidently, but not be able to sing starkers in front of your own teammates? After all, players need to have thick skin to deal with the media and fans.

***

At the end of my first year, Luton Town youth team won the league. We also reached the semi-final of the FA Youth Cup, losing to Leeds United over two legs. The Leeds team were excellent and had the likes of Alan Smith, Harry Kewell and Jonathan Woodgate in their squad. The quality of their football highlighted that I still had a lot of work to do.

Once the season ended, during the summer most of my team left to go on holiday with their families. That wasn't an option for me so I arranged to work with my uncle back up in Leith Docks. I spent the next six weeks lifting sand bags and mixing cement. It was good money, cash in hand, and a lot more than I was earning at the football club. When I came back for the new season, the dressing room chat was about holiday destinations and fun family time. When my turn came around, the place went quiet as I told everyone I'd been working. I got some strange looks and was asked if the coaches knew, because it was so unusual to work in the summer. But it had kept me out of trouble, I felt fit and strong, and I'd even managed to put some much-needed weight on.

Any chance I got, I would watch the first team players to see if I could pick up any tricks to copy. I found myself comparing my skills to theirs. The reserve team were holding their own in their league alongside Spurs, Arsenal and Chelsea reserve teams. If I could break into the reserve team I would have the opportunity to play against Premiership fringe players or world-class players coming back from suspension or injury.

I knew the second season of my apprenticeship was make or break. Most of the second years played quite a few games in the reserves and this gave the gaffer a chance to see if they could stand out amongst the professionals. After a midweek youth team game, John asked a couple of us how we'd feel about playing with the reserves the following day. It's unheard of in football to play a night match and then play the following afternoon. When we discovered it was against Spurs and they were putting out a strong team, Stuart and I looked at each other and grinned.

During the pre-match warm-up, I noticed a tall long-haired player alone on the centre spot casually juggling with the ball. He initially caught my eye because he was on his own and a team usually warms up together, but there was also something quite polished about him – which was when I realised it was the David Ginola. He was so relaxed. While everyone else was running around doing sprints, he just casually flicked the ball up and down effortlessly.

Stuart and I tossed a coin to see who would play which half. I won and chose the first. We had a fit technical player called Terry Sweeney going up against Ginola. It was the first time I'd had the privilege to watch the master at work in person. He never gave the ball away and Terry was snapping at his heels for 45 minutes like a Yorkshire terrier. This guy was in a league of his own. Every time Terry tried to pinch the ball off him, Ginola would spin out and send Terry the wrong way. It was a football master class. When the half-time whistle blew my legs were on fire, and I was more than happy to pass the reins to Stuart for the second half of the match. I suspected John had known that neither of us would be able to last the full duration of the game. I remember thinking how knackered Terry must have been, and I suspect he slept very well that night! Obviously Ginola's touch was phenomenal, but I was more amazed at the strength and physicality of him. He was pure muscle and after playing against him I wasn't surprised when he went on to win PFA Player of the Year later in the season.

10
Knock the Door Down

As my second season came to a head we won the South East Counties League Cup, beating West Ham in the final over two legs. They had two standout young players at the time, Joe Cole and Michael Carrick. In the first leg Matt Spring scored a wonder goal and Trésor Kandol got a hat trick for us at Upton Park, winning 4-0.

D-Day was approaching fast. This is the day when apprentices all over the country are told whether or not they have made the cut. It's go pro or go home. Everything I had been working towards for the last two years was building up to this one moment, so that morning when I was asked to step into the coaches' office I was extremely nervous. My heart was pounding in my ears. I sat down hardly daring to breathe. It felt like I was waiting for an eternity for someone to speak and tell me the news I desperately wanted to hear. They asked me a couple of questions about how I felt I'd done, then after a very long pause one of the coaches said I'd made the grade. They offered me a professional contract, and my wages jumped up dramatically. I was over the moon.

Gone were the days of cleaning toilets and fetching teas. I now had my own apprentice Darren Howe, who laid my kit out for me and cleaned my boots. I noticed that the banter in the first team dressing room was much more ruthless. It was extremely personal and unless you've been in the footballing world for a while and know what to expect, some of those comments would definitely get your back up.

Things were going great for me. Coming back from college on the train with Matt Spring one day, we got chatting to a brunette girl with lovely brown eyes called Louisa. As she left the train, she shouted her number out to us. Springy and I looked at each other because we genuinely didn't know which one of us she was directing it to, so we both wrote it down! Luckily for me, and maybe thanks to Springy's huge nose, Louisa became my first proper girlfriend.

Luton Town's first team were in Division Two, now known as League One. It was a strong division back then. We were up against Manchester City, Burnley, Stoke City and Fulham, to name just a few. John pulled me aside one day and asked me when I'd last spoken to the first team manager Lennie Lawrence. I shrugged my shoulders; I didn't know if I'd ever actually spoken to him. He told me to go and knock on his door every single week to tell him I wanted to be in the starting line-up for the first team. I looked at him as if he was mental. The gaffer had 30-odd players to choose from! He said that if I knocked every week it would show how hungry I was to play.

I thought about it for a bit and as I'm never one to turn down an opportunity I decided, fuck it. The following week I knocked on the gaffer's door and asked for a minute of his time. Probably a little overeager, I said I was ready to start. He told me not this week and to shut the door. I went back the next week, and the next week, and every week after that, asking exactly the same question, only to receive the same response. After a while I didn't even need to ask the question – as soon as the gaffer saw my face he'd say no. I didn't let up though. I was persistent.

One Thursday I knocked as usual and said the same thing I always said. I'd already started to turn around when I heard words I'd never heard coming from Lennie Lawrence's mouth before.

"You know what, son, you are ready. You're in the starting line-up for Saturday's game against Burnley."

I thought he was calling my bluff. My knocking had become a bit comical and I didn't really expect the gaffer to say yes, so when he did I wasn't prepared. I just stood in the doorway, so he told me to come in. I'd never been that far into his office before.

I'd only signed my first pro contract a few months before and I was so excited to be in the starting line-up. To this day, I'm still not sure if Lennie just put me in the team to stop me knocking on his door or if he actually felt I was ready to play!

I popped my head into John's office and told him the good news. He smiled at me and said he'd told me all that knocking would pay off. It's true, John was rarely wrong.

On match day, in the tunnel before the game I remember Mitchell Thomas and club captain Steve Davis pulling me aside to say, "Macca, listen, just run around and try to get on the ball as much as possible. Don't worry about making mistakes."

I made my home league debut for Luton Town on Saturday 5th September 1998 against Burnley at just 18 years old. I couldn't believe that only a few years ago I'd been kicking a ball against a shop shutter. I was buzzing.

The gaffer took me off after 81 minutes and I was incredibly emotional after receiving a standing ovation from the fans. We won 1-0. The game was everything I'd ever dreamed of. I played well and the experience boosted my belief in my ability. My adrenaline had been pumping all day from excitement, nerves and determination to prove myself on the pitch. I loved every minute of it. My older brother Martin called me from Scotland to congratulate me, which made it even better. The next morning I was hurting. I'd been bashed about a bit, but nothing could wipe the grin off my face.

I remember being on the pitch at an away game against Ipswich Town in the League Cup. There was only a matter of minutes before kick-off. Our striker at the time, Phil Gray, was stretching and jumping around on the centre spot getting ready to start. He called to me and when I looked over at him, he was standing in a lunge position looking down towards his foot. He was pissing all over the centre spot.

"What the fuck are you doing?" I said to him, trying not to laugh. It certainly took the edge off the impending match.

"I couldn't wait!" he yelled as the referee blew the

whistle and he nudged the ball into play.

Ipswich beat us 2-1. It was probably karma.

Within three months of making my first team debut and one day before my 19th birthday, Luton gave me a new and improved contract which doubled my salary. I was absolutely stunned as I'd only played 12 games! After working so hard for two years to get my first contract I wasn't expecting to be handed another so soon.

Later in the season we played against Manchester City at Maine Road. The atmosphere was comparable to what I used to experience watching Hearts play at Tynecastle Stadium. There were about 26,000 people there – the biggest crowd I'd ever faced. When the fans roared I got goosebumps. Each time Shaun Goater picked up the ball the Man City fans chanted, "Feed the Goat and he will score." He didn't, but Paul Dickov and Tony Vaughan did within the first ten minutes.

Towards the end of the game I remember Gavin McGowan running down the left wing chasing the ball as one of the Man City players went in for a tackle. They exchanged words with each other, as you do, but what came next really shocked me. The Man City player blatantly yelled, "You black cunt!"

Gavin went fucking ballistic and rightly so. The referee was at the other end of the pitch by now, so he missed it. I hadn't witnessed that kind of racist behaviour at any game between fellow professionals. We lost 2-0. After the match there were a few heated exchanges in the tunnel following the comments on the pitch.

One Friday before a home match, we were doing some shadow play; the first team passes the ball around on the pitch and the reserves have to shadow them as if they were the opposition but are not allowed to tackle in case of injury. During the session the ball went off the pitch for a throw-in. Playing for the reserves was a full back from the youth team. He went to take a throw-in and when the ball left his hands, it flew through the air like a heat-seeking missile, bypassing all the players. The gaffer immediately stopped the training session and, amazed, asked who this kid with the propeller arm was.

Jude Stirling had just been brought into the reserves for the day. What a way to get noticed. For the next ten minutes, the gaffer had us back in the 18-yard box defending Jude's throw-ins pretending they were corner kicks. The hardest part was trying to take up a position that anticipated where the ball was going to land. Jude's throw was extraordinary. It turned out he could lob the ball from the halfway line into the penalty box. He went on to become one of my best friends in football.

11
New Heart

On the pitch I was learning an incredible amount. In order to improve as a young player, you must master the art of decision-making. My development in awareness, body position and passing was definitely evolving. I felt I was beginning to understand my trade now that I was playing in professional matches. I wasn't selected every week, but that gave me something to work towards.

My increase in salary and bonuses for my first team appearances gave me more disposable income than I'd ever had before. I was taken aback. It was the largest amount of money I had ever earned in a single month. I was 19 and I didn't know what to do with myself. I bought a car and some new clothes. I also found myself with more free time as the first team trained less than I was accustomed to.

Back then a big drinking culture existed in football and being Scottish, I could certainly tuck a few away. I started to develop a problem with it and given my reckless youth, it wasn't surprising. The senior lads would take me to the casino with them. I was one of the youngest in the team, and I was mixing with seasoned professionals. In the past, I used to look up to drug dealers and heavy hitters. Now I looked up to professional footballers. Before I knew it, I was partying harder and drinking more than

I should have been. But it wasn't until the second year of my professional career that the partying had a noticeable effect. I'd slept late a couple of times, feeling hungover, turned up to training smelling of alcohol and the lads had been forced to throw me in a cold shower. I was drinking pretty much every other day, spinning out of control on an unconscious downward spiral.

I'd been with my teammate Gary Doherty on a night out in Dunstable when I was caught drink-driving; I was heading down the road the wrong way. After being charged with careless driving and drink-driving, a court date was set to determine my punishment. It was looking bad and there was a small chance I might be given a sentence. I kept it a secret from the club and from the lads. No one knew except Gary and my girlfriend's family, as a solicitor friend of theirs was representing me in court. My hearing was during training time, so I told the club I was at the dentist having a tooth removed. I hadn't really thought about what might happen if I were actually sent to prison!

When my turn came I was told to stand in the dock. My solicitor had warned me that there had been numerous cases of judges clamping down on drink-driving offences in order to set a precedent. It became quite tense at one point and during the awkward silence I rubbed my ankle against my leg, forgetting I was wearing my lucky Match of the Day football socks – the ones which, when you press the football pattern, play the familiar theme tune. Next thing I knew the entire courtroom was peering around to see where the noise was coming from. I felt so embarrassed and stared fixedly at my solicitor who was sitting opposite me. It was bastard timing. I managed to walk out with a £1,000 fine, a 12-month ban and I had to resit my test. I got lucky, no thanks to my socks, but from there on things went from bad to worse.

My girlfriend Louisa was sitting her exams at college and at the time her parents were going through a rough patch. She had enough going on and it didn't help that I was out on the piss nearly every night. John, who knew me very well by now, could also see that my drinking was an issue. When we sat down to discuss it, I lied when he asked me how many times per week I was going out. I said it was two nights a week, when really it was more like four. He knew I was lying but John always backed me, whereas Lennie told me I needed to take some time out. Somehow I managed to convince him to let me continue playing. But it got so bad they put a curfew on me, and the club's secretary would make sure I was tucked up in bed at my digs.

It started to piss some of the senior lads off; I was getting preferential treatment even though there was clearly a problem. They would get a fine or dropped from the team for putting a toe out of line. There were two incidents which struck a chord and highlighted how bad my problem was. I remember going out with the lads one night to Beach Nightclub, the usual haunt of the footballers in Luton Town. We were treated well and the venue massaged our egos. We were all downstairs having a drink when Trevor, the manager of the nightclub, came over and said my girlfriend was outside in her pyjamas crying. I ran upstairs to find out what the fuck was going on. She was sobbing hysterically. She told me her parents had been arguing and it had turned sour. I knew it must be bad for her to come and find me like this.

I hated her old man. I thought he was weak. I would have handled the situation differently if I hadn't been drinking but because I'd had a few, I was really fired up. I didn't like seeing Louisa so upset. She was a lovely girl and her mum didn't deserve to be treated like that. I thought he needed a taste of his own medicine. I went straight to the house, dragged her old man outside and laid into him. I'm not proud of what I did. I'd lowered myself to his level, but in my drunken haze I thought I was doing the right thing.

Someone from Louisa's family called the football club the next day to try to have me sacked. I thought I'd helped the situation and that Louisa's dad would lay off her mum now. Obviously I hadn't helped. John called me into his office to talk about the complaint.

"Give me one good reason why I shouldn't sack you on the spot, son."

I mulled over my reply. I didn't want to betray Louisa's trust and divulge her family's affairs, but I had to explain the full story to John. He told me to get back to training; he knew me well enough to realise I wouldn't have behaved in such a manner if I hadn't felt it was in some way justified. Unfortunately my relationship with Louisa was never the same again and we broke up, but we did stay in regular contact.

A few months later my curfew was lifted and I decided to go out with some student friends. I had a game the next day. It wasn't unusual to be recognised by football fans in the town, but as it was the night before a game I tried to remain incognito by wearing a hat. It's written into most football contracts that players are not allowed to frequent licensed premises 48 hours prior to a match. A player can be fined up to two weeks' wages or even sacked for such an offence.

I was tucked away in the corner of a bar when a girl came over. She wasn't a supermodel but she looked okay, and I was single again. We had a chat and a few hours later I went home to bed very drunk. The next afternoon I arrived at Kenilworth Road and made my way to the dressing room. Lennie Lawrence came in as normal to announce the team, but just before he did, he told us he'd received information that one of us had been out on the piss last night. He reiterated how unacceptable this behaviour was, but he'd give the person a chance to own up. The dressing room fell silent. I could feel the alcohol sweating out of my pores and my face growing red. I could have sworn I hadn't been recognised.

Nobody said a word. The gaffer turned to face me and asked where I'd been last night. I froze. I didn't know what to say. I tried to make light of it by saying I'd just popped out for a couple of beers. He lost it and told me to fuck off out of the dressing room. He said he would deal with me on Monday.

It turned out that the girl I'd been chatting up worked for a local newspaper and she had called the club with the story.

I returned on Monday morning for a meeting with Lennie and Cherry Newbery, the club secretary. They had a serious chat with me. They were sending me for an assessment because they were adamant I had a problem. It wasn't a choice; it was comply or lose my job.

The following day I went to Southampton with one of the fitness coaches, Mandy, to speak to a doctor. I didn't have a clue where we were going until we pulled up outside the Priory. I'd heard of other footballers and celebrities being sent there to sort out personal issues. I sat with the doctor who asked me when the last time was that I hadn't had a drink. I didn't answer because I genuinely couldn't remember.

Honestly, at the time I couldn't see what the problem was. I'm Scottish and I'd been drinking since I was ten years old. Everyone I knew in Scotland drank like a trooper. Going over the last few weeks' events allowed me to recognise that my behaviour amounted to a sackable offence. And it was only when the doctor asked me if my friends or the people close to me were affected by my drinking that I realised I could actually have a problem. They told me I needed to stay there for a month. It was December 1999 and I was going to be in there for the turn of the millennium. I was gutted but more than that, I felt apprehensive about what was to come.

Initially I told the doctor I couldn't stay and that I

would come back after Christmas, but he said he had strict instructions from my manager that I either completed the full month's course or I would never play football for them again. It was my choice to make. He pointed out that Paul Gascoigne had sat in the very same chair that I was in. He hadn't listened. The doctor said that my boss believed I had a bright future, and he had given me more chances than I probably deserved. I didn't disagree with that fact and I committed to do the full course and return two days later.

On the way back Mandy pointed out that being part of the football industry, whether I liked it or not, made me a role model for others. This fact really resonated with me. I'd spent much of my own youth looking up to the wrong kind of people, and the realisation that young kids might look at me in the same way hit me hard. I didn't want other kids to see my recent behaviour as acceptable. It gave me a hell of a lot to think about.

The discussion turned to my late arrival at training a few days earlier, with Mandy trying to make light of the situation. Bless her. She was laughing at me but I couldn't understand why because at the time I'd received another bollocking from Lennie. I'd woken up late after a drink-fuelled night, jumped in the car and as I pulled into the training ground, saw that the lads were already warming up, doing a lap of the pitch. Thinking quickly (or so I thought), I noticed they were approaching the bushes by the car park. I figured I could sneak through the bushes to join in with the lads doing the lap. The coaches were on the other side of the pitch so they probably wouldn't see me; they would just assume I'd been there all along. As I sneaked in amongst the other players, one of the lads noticed me and asked where I'd been. I told him I'd had one too many beers last night and I'd overslept. He asked why I'd even bothered to turn up, and I should have just said I was sick. I was confused.

Then I realised it wasn't the warm-up; it was the fucking warm-down! The lads had been training for over an hour.

Mandy said the coaches had actually seen me pull up in the car. They'd found watching me crawl through the bushes hilarious, but nevertheless they'd had to take a serious stance on it. Lennie and John had told me to leave my car at the training ground and run in my football boots for two miles back up to the stadium. They hadn't actually thought I would accept the punishment and do as I was told. She said it had made them laugh even more. I really appreciated that she was trying to make me feel better, but the episode was a bit of a blur and just hearing her talk about it made me cringe. It was dawning on me that I might really have a serious drinking problem.

Mandy dropped me back in Southampton at Marchwood Priory as promised on Friday 17th December 1999. I'd just turned 20. Nobody knew I was going in, not even my mum or my brother.

I still wasn't completely sure what this place was or what to expect. The same doctor who had assessed me previously now greeted me. I went through some forms with him, including a confidentiality agreement.

They explained to me again that I had to complete the 28-day course and if they were happy with my progress, I would be allowed to return to football. Once we'd finished, they escorted me to another room. I could hear people cheering. As they opened the door I could see about eight people standing in a circle singing and holding hands.

I stood watching the sight in front of me, genuinely thinking I was in a loony bin! It was probably the last thing I was expecting to see. The words 'cult' and 'crazy' sprung to mind. I looked at the doctor and asked if Mandy had left already. He just nudged me further into the room and shut the door. I looked at the group of singing people and realised there was a familiar football face in the circle, Adam Tanner. He was playing for Ipswich Town at the time. I remembered him scoring the winning goal during his debut at Anfield, but I had also played against him last season. Seeing a football face there eased my anxiety.

I was woken up at 6am every morning and put through intense psychology sessions until around 9pm. Initially I was extremely uncomfortable talking about my personal issues in front of random strangers. The first few days felt like an eternity. On several occasions I thought about packing my bag and leaving, but each time something inside told me to stay.

During my first week, the doctor said somebody had arrived to give me some much-needed advice. I duly waited in my room. I heard a knock at the door and as it opened I was definitely not prepared to see the face that appeared. It was Paul Merson, as in *the* Paul Merson, the Arsenal and England legend, standing in my room, wanting to give me advice.

Once I had overcome my initial shock, I discovered Merse had been in the Priory previously and as we spoke he was evidently very grounded. I found it easy to talk to him about the whole situation because he understood how I felt. The moment he told me I was a lucky bastard, though, I actually wanted to punch him in the face. I didn't understand what he meant and I was stupidly feeling sorry for myself. He went on to explain that because I was in here at a younger age than he had been, it meant I could fix my problem a lot sooner. Merse went on to tell me that the PFA had asked him to talk to me and that he'd also had a chat with Luton Town.

When I finally understood what he meant, I realised that, yes, I was lucky. I was very lucky. All these people actually gave a shit about my problem and wanted to help me sort it out.

If it had been anyone other than Merse saying this to me, I don't think I would have felt the same way, but because he was such a legend it was much more potent. I literally hung on to every word he said. Who better to give someone like me advice? And it meant more knowing that he'd been through a similar battle but had still managed to play at the level he had. I could relate to some of his stories. Merse laughed when I recalled my first encounter with the singing circle; the same initial sight had freaked him out too.

After speaking to Merse I felt much more positive about the challenges that lay ahead. I decided to embrace the programme more fully and to open up about some of my past demons.

Due to the confidentiality agreement I signed, I cannot discuss my time there in too much detail. What I will say, though, is being there forced me to really analyse my life and the choices I had made. My sessions with the psychologists helped me to delve deeper, to look at why I might be lashing out like this and pressing the self-destruct button.

I'd been drinking since the age of ten, so it had become part of my daily routine. Coming from Scotland, where the majority of people drink copious amounts of alcohol, to go against that culture would be abnormal. You'd be like a fucking alien up north if you didn't drink. I don't think there was ever a day that went by when my father or uncles weren't in the pub. It was a normal and accepted part of the society I was born into.

I couldn't understand the difference between having a couple of drinks to unwind and getting blind drunk. I'm an all-or-nothing type of person with a highly addictive personality. It's deemed a 'man thing' to be able to drink someone under the table. I suppose it feels like a compliment to have someone admit you can tuck a few away. Also, until the turn of the millennium footballers were never thought of as athletes. There was a huge drinking culture amongst players.

Now, having met many people from outside the

estate, I can recognise that my childhood was actually quite fucked up. Never having a stable background but instead being left free to run wild, meant I never really had to think about anyone else or what the consequences of my actions might be. On the estate no one gave a fuck, but now there were people that did. I had my career to think about and my actions did affect everyone around me. Every bad decision had a repercussion. I just hadn't realised it until then. My sessions at the Priory made me see that simply turning up to training late was disruptive to the team. I saw how selfish I was being.

I didn't know it at the time but spending those 28 days in the Priory was the best thing that ever happened to me. It's not a guaranteed fix for everybody; there are some people who have come out only to fall off the wagon again. For me, I came out in a strong spiritual state with a focus that was much needed for my future career and life. I left the Priory with a very different perspective and a renewed outlook. It felt like they had removed my heart and fitted me with a new one.

I cannot thank the staff at the Priory enough for the help they gave me during the month I was there – and, more importantly, John Moore, Lennie Lawrence, the board and all the back-room staff at Luton Town FC for recognising my problem for me. I will always be tremendously grateful to them.

Once I came out, I knew life wouldn't be normal again, because before my stint in rehab, 'normal' for me was to drink every day. It was hard. Each day was its own battle. Merse offered to be my sponsor and became a huge inspiration to me over the coming years. Thankfully he was there at the end of the phone whenever I needed to talk to him. He could relate to how I was feeling, so he gave me good and relevant advice. He wasn't the only one. A few people sent me cards or messages. TV presenter Nick Owen, who is now the chairman of Luton Town, and his family sent me a lovely personal note.

I returned to training at Luton Town. The press got wind of where I'd been and, as they do, wrote shit. All I could do was take one day at a time. My teammates saw a change in me. The PFA was happy with my progress and I spoke to John about where I stood. Lennie still had me on the bench; there were only a few months left in the season and he didn't think I was mentally ready yet. I took it on the chin. He was good about it, though, and very encouraging. He told me I just needed to get my head back on the game, refocus and, more importantly, stay away from the drink. I was only 20 after all.

We were playing Colchester at home. I was on the bench. We were winning 1-0 when the referee blew his whistle for half-time. The home fans started to boo the referee. Walking across the pitch towards the tunnel, I remember saying to one of the lads that I didn't think the referee had had that bad a half to be booed. As I reached the tunnel entrance, a couple of fans spat on me. I was pushed up the tunnel before I could react, but I was fucking fuming. It wasn't the referee the fans were booing. It was me! They still had a lot of anger they were directing towards me for having taken the piss out of their club before going into the Priory. It was the first time I'd felt their wrath and it wasn't a good feeling.

Lennie pulled me in that week. He was under pressure. Even though I'd completed the course I knew he was going to tell me my time was up at the club. He told me they'd pay the rest of my wages in advance but I needed a fresh start somewhere else. I felt truly disappointed. I was really hoping to get back on track at Luton. I loved the club. I knew I would miss the staff, especially John. During my time there he had been my mentor; his training had shaped the player I had become and I really looked up to him. I would even miss the gaffer! I wasn't angry with Lennie; it was a tough decision and I understood. That's the nature of the game, but I just didn't realise it would be so soon after rehab. It was a massive blow.

I had made some good friends there, particularly Jude Stirling. He wasn't a big drinker so I'd been spending a lot of time with him. Jude was shocked when I told him I was out, but he told me to find a new club and keep my head down.

I was at a loose end because the current season still had a couple of months left to go, and I was filled with a mixture of emotions. I kept my head down, switched off my phone and made the most of some thinking time. I toyed with all sorts of ideas about what to do next but always came back to the same answer. I wanted to carry on playing football. It was my dream. If I could play in Division Two pissed, imagine how far I could go sober.

After all, five years ago, I would never have dreamed that I could sign a professional contract. I didn't know how to go about getting a new club as I didn't have an agent at the time. My head was all over the place so I decided to just get on with the next few months. I spent some time with friends in Harpenden in Hertfordshire. My mate was dating a girl whose father, Tony Golder, was a big Luton fan. He knew I was trying to get back on my feet and kindly offered to let me stay with him for a bit. His family were unbelievably generous to me and I helped out with some gardening to earn my keep. Sometime in June, Tony came out to the garden to tell me I had a call. I was a bit shocked. I hadn't turned my phone on for a while and no one knew I was at Tony's.

"Are you sure they mean me?" I asked.

"I'm telling you, it's for you," Tony replied. I walked into the kitchen and took the phone.

"Hello?"

"Hi Michael."

12
Lifeline

I couldn't believe I'd just spoken to the scout Ron Jukes on the phone. Hereford United wanted me to play for them next season. It was a drop of two divisions, but I didn't hesitate in agreeing to meet him and agent Lorraine Gates the next day. We met at a hotel just off the M5. I signed a no-nonsense contract on the spot. If I fucked about I was out. I thought that was fair. Drinking was the last thing I wanted to do. The money wasn't great but it wasn't about that, I just wanted to play again.

Ron, bless him, has passed away now, but when he was writing his book he asked me to contribute to it. I talked about how I had come to know Ron and that I still have no idea how he ever managed to find me. I asked him but he never told me. How Ron tracked me down to Tony's doesn't matter because, thanks to him, I had the lifeline I needed to kick-start my football career again.

At the time of my arrival in July 2000, Hereford United was in the Football Conference. Graham Turner was not only Hereford's manager but also the chairman. Many people doubled up on jobs. Ian Rodgerson drove the minibus, was the physio and played with the team. Considering the meagre resources Graham had at Hereford, it was a very well-run club and ruthlessly organised. I take my hat off to him as he did a great job. Being the manager of a football club is stressful enough, let alone being the chairman too!

Hereford is quiet, so it was the perfect place to help me stay out of trouble. Graham put me in digs in a farmhouse run by Eileen and Wally, with some other players, Gavin Williams, Chris Lane, Matt Baker and Andy Moran. It was miles from anywhere so once we were in after training that was it; there was nowhere to go and zero distractions. For young lads, the setup they provided for us was perfect. Chris and Andy were from Liverpool and Gav was from Merthyr Tydfil, whereas Matt was from Harrogate and very posh in comparison. (He actually went on to be a very active Conservative Party member.) It was a funny mixture but what a good bunch of lads. We worked and lived together, so inevitably we became close. It turned out to be exactly the fresh start I needed.

I was probably closest to Gav out of all the lads I lived with, and apart from Jackie McNamara and Ally McCoist, Gav is probably one of the funniest footballers you will ever meet. We became good friends and eventually went on to play together at three different clubs. I developed a kind of telepathic relationship with him on the pitch – we just clicked. We could have played football blindfolded and still known where the other was throughout the match. This doesn't happen a lot in football; in fact, it's extremely rare. The fact that we were two players making the same split-second decisions 90% of the time provided us with a huge advantage. The movement off the ball becomes so predictable to the player on the ball that it gives the opposition less time to react. For instance, if I was trying to pick an eye-of-the-needle pass through the defence, I'd know exactly what Gav would be thinking and what weight of pass he would like before he even moved. Later, we shared an old saying: "It doesn't matter what country, what league, what stadium we played in, we could influence the result of any game."

One of my first games for Hereford United was against local rivals Shrewsbury Town in a pre-season friendly. My introduction to the non-league world gave me a short, sharp shock as Mickey Brown headbutted me during the match. It turned into a mass brawl with most of the players getting involved. Five minutes later I was smashed again, this time by David Hughes. It finished 0-0 but the game was far from boring.

In our digs we used to fight over who got to read the weekly Non-League Paper first. It did a great job of recognising and bringing to the public's attention the lower leagues. The beauty of non-league football is that it's purely about the game and isn't clouded by money. Playing at that level really opened my eyes to the talent on show in the Football Conference. One of the big turning points in English football was when Sky began to show live coverage of Conference League matches, giving the lower leagues a much-needed financial boost.

On 19th August 2000 I made my debut at home for Hereford against Southport. We drew 0-0. The Hereford fans were incredibly passionate. The club pulled in around

2,000 fans a week, which is a great turnout for such a small city.

With nothing to distract me, all I did was train, eat and sleep. I had stayed in regular contact with my ex-girlfriend Louisa. She was now studying at Manchester University and managed to get a part-time job working at Old Trafford, serving the players their pre-match meals. I used to call her after every weekend to find out what each player ate before the match. For example, when David Beckham was scoring goals, Louisa told me he was eating strawberries and yoghurt as part of his pre-match meal. So guess what I would eat the following week!

On top of this I began training once a week at Dorian Yates' gym in Birmingham to bulk up. On one occasion I trained with Dorian Yates himself, who had won Mr Olympia six consecutive times. He was an absolute mountain and until I saw him in action with my own eyes, I would never have believed a human being could lift so much.

I also did my weightlifting sessions with Commonwealth Games gold medallist Tony Ford. He specialised in improving the team's strength and conditioning and he tailored workouts for me. I was getting stronger and developing a speed I'd never known before. Graham put me in a new position, left wing. We had a good team and some decent players like Gav, Paul Parry, Phil Robinson, Matt Clarke, Tony James and Scott Cooksey. We were becoming one of the most physical teams in the league.

A couple of months into the 2000/01 season, Wolves

legend Steve Bull arrived. I think he was doing his coaching badges at the time, but he played six games with us and still showed glimpses of incredible talent. He would roll you in training and score in the bottom corner every single time. Control, turn, bottom corner. I can only imagine what he was like at the peak of his career if he was still playing like that at the age of 36.

Tony Ford's pre-match team talk was something reminiscent of an American football team's. He would get all the lads running on the spot and down doing press-ups to pump their muscles. At this point Gav used to take the piss, sneak off and hide in the shower. Then our centre midfielder and captain John Snape, a physically strong player, would walk around the dressing room, shake your hand and headbutt you. Not enough to crack a skull but enough to wind you up before the game! After taking a rap to the head, the lads would run out onto the pitch with their adrenaline racing. Not exactly a normal pre-match routine, but it worked for us.

Graham Turner called me to his office to tell me that Steve Evans from Boston United FC had been in touch to make an offer for me of around £20,000. I was gobsmacked. Boston United was also in the Football Conference at the time but I hadn't even considered a move. He told me to sleep on it but that Hereford United was a selling club and the offer was good for them. The club would make a profit on me and they were keen to get the deal done, but the final decision was mine. I got up, shook his hand and left his office. I went home and talked it through with the lads.

I really didn't know what to do. I analysed my options. Would the move benefit me that much, as Boston was in the same league? Although they were one of the higher paying clubs in the division, I was happy at Hereford. I felt settled here so I was undecided.

The following day I went to see the gaffer again to discuss it some more. He'd had another offer, this time from Yeovil Town FC for £25,000. This changed things, as they were at the top of the league. I'd only been here for seven months, but this was the first time that a club had wanted to buy me – let alone two clubs!

In the Conference you were never talking crazy sums of money. There weren't huge salaries or big transfer fees. Financially, a move to Boston United made better sense for me as my wages would be higher. It wasn't just about the money, though; I had a plan. Graham would make more profit on me if I chose Yeovil. It was a decent amount then for a club at that level. I felt I owed that much to Hereford United as they had done so much for me during my short time there, and it would possibly get me back into the Football League quicker. At the last minute I rang Merse to make sure I was doing the right thing. He told me it was a good move, to sign, go and not look back. I told Graham I would like to go to Yeovil Town and the deal was done for £25,000.

We had a game coming up that Saturday against Hednesford Town and the gaffer asked if I would play one last match with the team. I said absolutely. We won the match 3-0 so it was the perfect way to say goodbye to the

Hereford United team. I thanked all the staff, especially Graham who joked that he needed to sell me to pay the floodlight electricity bill. He probably did! I felt I owed him a lot. He'd given me the perfect platform I needed to step up and play. It was a tad emotional as we man hugged, but it felt good to leave on a positive note. Graham put a great deal of time into footballers with personal problems; I always admired him for that. The worst bit was leaving the digs. I'd built a strong bond with the lads there and I was genuinely gutted to leave them.

I still hold Hereford United close to my heart as this was the team that helped me back onto the footballing ladder, and Graham provided me with everything I needed to do this. He's a great bloke and I will always be grateful to him for his understanding, his confidence in my ability, and most of all his kindness. There were no judgements at Hereford. Lennie Lawrence had been right. I did need a new club to drive me forward and allow my football to do the talking.

13
Camaraderie

At Yeovil Town, I was signed by manager Colin Addison. I'd heard good things about Colin beforehand; people said he had a vast knowledge of the game. At that time Yeovil seemed very ambitious. On the drive down I asked myself what I expected to achieve from this club – obviously to get promoted and get my arse back into the Football League. I was still young but needed to make up some lost time. So based on what I'd learned at the Priory, I put a ten-year plan in place.

Like every professional footballer, the aim is to play in the Premiership and of course to have a place in your national team. Mine was no different. I had a long climb up the ladder but as long as I was promoted each season or got a move while doing well at the club I was playing for, I would be happy. I had no more time to fuck about and so I set my sights on being the best athlete I could be. No alcohol (obviously) and no shit food.

It had been a quick turnaround as my new gaffer wanted me to play in the coming Saturday's match. On Saturday 17th February 2001 I made my debut on the left wing for Yeovil Town at Huish Park, funnily enough against Boston United, and scored my first goal in the 43rd minute. We won 2-1 and I got Man of the Match. I knew then I'd definitely made the right choice and bearing in mind that Yeovil Town's transfer fee for me was then a club record, I think they were pretty happy too.

I moved into a flat, only a couple of minutes' drive from the ground, with teammates Ben Smith and club captain Terry Skiverton.

I'd come to Yeovil while they were at the top of the league. The team were seven points clear of second place Rushden & Diamonds and were tipped to win the only promotion spot available. The atmosphere at games was brilliant, but then somehow it all went wrong and we lost some of our key players to injury. Towards the end of the season we had one fit striker and the gaffer had to put central defenders in attacking positions. The pitch at Huish Park didn't help either. It was horrendous. There was no drainage and a third of it was like a beach; you could unexpectedly lose your boot in the sand while running with the ball.

We even lost to Hereford 3-2. Within a matter of matches Rushden & Diamonds steamed ahead of us and we finished in 2nd place, six points behind them. On the last day of the season I remember walking around the stadium thinking the bastard pitch had cost us our promotion. The next day the gaffer resigned. It came as a bit of a surprise but I think there were some differences between him and the board.

Yeovil Town appointed Gary Johnson as the new manager for the new 2001/02 season. When I was at Luton Town, GJ had been on the coaching staff at Watford and previously had managed the Latvian national team. I could see quite quickly that he wanted to mix up the squad and offload some of our current team. He brought in his son Lee Johnson and a few players from the reserve team at Watford. I hadn't been in this position before, where the manager who'd signed me had then gone on to leave, so I was a bit apprehensive about what would happen next. I still had another two years left on my contract.

During GJ's first couple of weeks at the club he absolutely tore into every one of us, particularly me. He came into Yeovil like a bull in a china shop. Now that I know GJ, it's safe to say he has a unique and influential style of managing.

Lee Johnson was definitely one of the lads. I got on well with him; he was my 'roomy' at away games. He wasn't oversensitive and the lads could have a laugh with him about his dad being the manager. Lee was also sometimes a good go-between. I had a chat with him about GJ constantly being on my case. I thought I was performing well. Lee told me that his dad did this at every new club. He'd pick on people to push them to their limits to see if they'd quit. It was a test to find out what your character was like.

Now armed with beneficial information, I changed my tactics. Rather than rising to the bait every time he yelled at me, I just gave him the thumbs up before he could finish. It's difficult to argue with someone if they think you're agreeing with them.

Once GJ knew he had you on board, he gave you the

freedom to express yourself. He was ruthless but in a good way and introduced strict rules across the club. Players had to live within a couple of miles of the training ground, which actually worked well because it meant we really got to know one another. We always went to Kirk Jackson's on a Monday night for pizza. Spending time together on and off the pitch naturally meant that the team became closer. Based on the number of teams I have been a part of in my career, none of them have been as tight as the team at Yeovil under GJ. Normally in football there's a fight or argument every other day due to the overabundance of male ego flying around, but GJ managed to create a harmonious team, which started to show that season.

GJ didn't create a sense of hierarchy at the club. Everyone was equal on and off the pitch. He encouraged the players to mix with fans and spend money in the town, helping to boost the community spirit. He let us out on a Friday night before a home match, providing we were home by 7pm. All the players would go to the same Italian restaurant and have a meal together. We'd eat, split the bill then as we left, beep our car horns. Most managers don't want you out at all before a match, but GJ trusted us not to take the piss and to be home on time, which in fairness to the lads we always did. We just 'carbed up' ready for our next game.

GJ also brought in top psychologist Mark Lader. I hadn't worked with anyone in that capacity since coming out of the Priory. Most footballers have the attention span of a goldfish. Mark trained us to focus for longer. Using the techniques he taught us, I was able to look at removing impurities from my life so that I could focus solely on my goals. GJ did a proper job of positively shaking up the club and our place within the community too. By implementing all these changes he managed to attract more fans to the home matches. But the best thing he did for the club was persuading the board to agree to a new pitch. It was then that we started to win matches easily. Under GJ we had evolved as a squad and there was a noticeable improvement in our individual and team performance. We were settled.

In my opinion Gary Johnson's professionalism and his approach towards the game and how it should be played were his greatest strengths as a manager. He rarely drank and always tried to bring in players with that same mindset, which worked well for me. His motto was along the lines of: "Don't sign players who you need to motivate. Sign players who motivate you."

14
Stanno

We signed Adam Stansfield from Elmore FC in the lower leagues. Adam went on to play an integral role that season, helping us to reach the final of the FA Trophy and finishing 3rd in the league. He took to the club's philosophy like a duck to water. He had bundles of energy for a striker, and any opposing defence would only have seconds on the ball before Adam hunted them down.

A few days before the FA Trophy Cup final against Stevenage at Villa Park, we travelled to the ground to familiarise ourselves with the place. Club psychologist Mark decided to take Adam into an empty press conference room to ask him what he would like the outcome to be for Sunday's match.

Adam told him he wanted to score, pick up Man of the Match and get his hands on the trophy. Mark suggested recreating how the press conference would go after the match if he managed to achieve all of these things. Agreeing, Adam took a seat in front of the sponsorship boards and, as if he were a journalist, Mark fired questions at him about how he felt winning Man of the Match, scoring his goal and lifting the trophy.

The objective of what seemed like Mark's madness was to entice Adam's subconscious to visualise and believe his dreams. If done properly this can be a very powerful tool, especially in sport. When Mark first joined the club many people were sceptical about his methods but it didn't take long before the whole squad was hanging onto his every word.

On Sunday 12th May 2002, in Adam's biggest game to date, he went on to score in the 66th minute, win Man of the Match and lift the FA trophy for Yeovil Town just as Mark had made him believe he would. After the game Adam took the same seat he'd sat in 48 hours earlier – this time, though, for real in front of a packed press conference.

***

Tragically Adam passed away in August 2010 at the tender age of 31 from bowel cancer. My lasting memory of Adam will always be the look of pure happiness on his face that day, in that press conference at Villa Park.

15
Making History

Just before we broke for the summer, GJ asked my opinion on signing my mate Gavin Williams from Hereford. I told him it was a good idea, particularly as we worked so well together. I knew if GJ ever needed to, he could sell Gav on easily because he was such a good player. Gav came on board and moved in next door to me.

Winning the FA Trophy had kick-started the team's mindset towards a winning mentality. And our chances of winning the league increased at the start of the new season when the FA introduced a new play-off system, meaning that an extra team could be promoted. Rolling into the 2002/03 season, we were unstoppable. The technical ability and fitness levels of the team, along with our speed and attacking skills, were way above Conference level. This was proven as many of the team went on to play in higher divisions.

As the team clicked, Yeovil went from strength to strength. I felt like each of us was giving our all to the team. GJ and Mark's positive mindset swept through the dressing room. Lee Johnson would bring in a CD of Al Pacino's speech from the film 'Any Given Sunday', which he blasted at full volume before every match as part of our team talk. Any sporting person could relate to those words. It's one of the greatest inspirational sporting speeches of all time.

When a team is on a winning streak you tend to stick to the same superstitious routine, as you don't want to run the risk of doing anything different in case you break that line of success. As I said, before every home game the entire team would meet at the Italian restaurant on the Friday night and beep our horns as we left. Then first thing the next morning, several of the lads would meet at my place for a glass of apple and carrot juice before heading to the ground. It sounds mad but we didn't lose a league match at Huish Park all season.

I remember Nick Crittenden, our right wing back, and I having a chat with Yeovil Town's owner at the time, Jon Goddard-Watts (and also the brain behind Screwfix), about his beautiful yellow Lamborghini. We joked that if we were able finish the season with 40 goals between us, we should be allowed to have a go in his car. He told us he'd give us his Lamborghini if we could achieve that many goals. Before he could change his mind we shook his hand and used that as an incentive to score as many as we possibly could.

The new pitch had made such a difference. The ball now slid across the surface at lightning speed; we were passing teams off the pitch. The stands were full and we had set the bar so high that whenever we didn't maintain the standard, the fans (rightly so) would lay into us. Lee, being the manager's son, used to get it from them first and I remember one away game in particular against Boston United when Lee, by his own standards, was having an absolute horror show. He was taking some serious stick from the Yeovil fans. He told me afterwards that things had been so bad during the match that he'd seriously considered faking an epileptic fit (even though he doesn't have epilepsy) just so the physio would take him off. I laughed so much. He ended up getting a red card and was sent off after 90 minutes. We lost 4-2.

On Lee's good days he played a pivotal part in the team's structure and acted as the feeder. Everything went through Lee – good, bad and indifferent – not only behind the scenes but more importantly on the pitch, through his centre midfield position. He would always feed the ball to me or Gav. Alongside Lee was Darren Way. He was only 5ft 5in but could jump 8ft and had an endless supply of energy.

***

In the dressing room I had overheard a conversation between some of the lads about the previous afternoon when they'd gone for a Sunday roast with their families to a local pub restaurant. During the meal some dickhead punters had hurled abuse at the players in front of their wives and young children. They felt embarrassed by the situation but hadn't wanted to cause a scene while they were with their families.

Collectively, as we all lived in the town, the team made sure we ate in local restaurants and despite what other people may think about football, there is no denying that when a club is doing well it has a ripple effect throughout the entire town or city. The whole club had put a great deal of effort into working with the community to help bring it together. It was a piss-take that the lads had been out having a quiet meal and had had to endure treatment like that. Even though I hadn't been there, I took the news personally and was really annoyed.

After training, I drove over to the pub to speak to some of the locals to find out what had happened. They confirmed that a group of men had been giving them grief during their meal for a good 20 minutes. They agreed that the players had shown a lot of restraint and in the end had chosen to leave. I was told that these blokes were regulars and usually drank there later in the week. A few days after, Gav and I drove up there but nobody was around. Later on, though, one of the locals called to say that the same blokes were in the pub but this time there were quite a few more of them.

There have been many times on and off the pitch over the years when Gav and I have had to watch each other's backs. He's the kind of person who, if you were going to war, you'd want him in the trenches with you. Being from Merthyr Tydfil in Wales, Gav is definitely no shrinking violet.

I called a friend of mine who was a huge fan of the team and football in general. He lived locally and had a good idea who these blokes were. He suggested he should come with us to have a chat with them, so I went to pick him up. Gav also spoke to one of the other players and mentioned we were going up there.

As we pulled up at the pub I couldn't believe that the entire football team had turned up; a full 20-man squad had amassed. The lads in my car got out, along with one of the players who had been there on that Sunday so that he could identify the blokes. We told the rest of the boys to wait outside.

What happened next was like a scene out of an old Western movie. Let's just say, I don't think those blokes will ever abuse another one of their town's footballers again in a hurry.

The following day it was agreed that we would speak to Mark, the club psychologist, to see whether he felt we should let GJ know what had happened, in case the media got wind of it. He said we should wait until after our match in a few days' time, to catch the gaffer in a good mood – providing, of course, we won the match. Despite what had happened, Mark was impressed that the whole team had stuck together and was sure that the gaffer would feel the same way. Luckily for us we did win our match and Mark was right, GJ understood.

***

By October we were at the top of the league, and I was delighted to sign a new contract with the club. By February we were still at the top, 11 points clear of Chester City. By April we were smashing every team and 14 points clear of Doncaster Rovers, having played 38 out of 42 games. On

12th April 2003 we had an away game against Doncaster, and Chester City were up against Woking – their result would determine whether we'd won the league before we even kicked off.

We travelled up to Doncaster who, in fairness to them, had also had a strong season. Their chairman John Ryan had been busy pumping a lot of money into the team to give them a better chance of getting promoted.

While the lads were out warming up at Belle Vue I asked GJ if I could stay and listen to what was happening between Chester and Woking. So Steve Thompson, our coach, GJ and I were together when the news came through that Chester had drawn 2-2 with Woking – meaning that we had won the Football Conference! The feeling of elation, knowing that we'd bagged the league title with four games still to go, was indescribable. It was an incredible feeling! I will never forget the feeling of euphoria we shared that day. I remember Steve, GJ and me yelling and jumping around before I realised that my game was about to be shown live on Sky and I needed to get my arse out to warm up.

I ran out to the lads on the pitch who still weren't aware of the amazing news. But the loyal Yeovil away fans soon let their team know that we were champions. The atmosphere at Belle Vue that day was phenomenal.

It was such a surreal feeling knowing we'd already won the league. We beat Doncaster Rovers 4-0 with goals from Darren Way, Lee Johnson, Kevin Gall and myself from the penalty spot. All our adrenaline and happiness went into that one game. It was a sweet end to the day.

With three more games to go, Nick and I still had the owner's yellow Lamborghini in our sights. By the end of the season we'd managed 22 goals between us, so unfortunately we were still short of our 40-goal target. However as a team in those last few games we accumulated 18 goals, leading us to break the Conference record at the time. That season I scored 13 goals.

For the first time in 108 years, Yeovil Town FC ended the season on the ultimate high as champions of the Football Conference, with a record 17-point margin, accumulating a total of 95 points and scoring 100 goals, remaining unbeaten in the league at home all season. It was an extraordinary achievement.

In my first full season at Yeovil Town, we'd won the FA Trophy, which in itself was a fantastic accolade for the club, and finished 3rd in the Football Conference. In the second season we smashed Conference records and were crowned champions.

I absolutely loved playing at Yeovil. We'd won because of GJ, the support from his staff, and the new pitch he'd insisted we have installed. His style of management was the best thing that had happened to that club and he'd put together a team that flourished under his methods. I've never played with a team so tightly integrated and settled, which gave us the freedom to express our creativity. I was ecstatic to be part of the history we created.

Maintaining tradition, we went out to celebrate in the open-top bus. I was so happy for everyone involved. It meant so much to so many people. Considering they were based in the middle of nowhere, and the size of the town, the club had such a loyal following.

Once the season had ended and while we were still enjoying our success, I attended an awards ceremony in Blackpool as I'd been nominated for the Conference Player of the Year. I felt very privileged and enormously proud. I'd knuckled down and battled through my demons.

I went up with GJ, who had also been nominated for Manager of the Year. I remember the award ceremony as if it was yesterday. Sticking to my Scottish roots, I hired a kilt especially for the occasion. It was mainly managers and chairmen in attendance from all 22 football clubs in the Football Conference.

When my category came around, I won and was named Conference Player of the Year 2002/03. It was an absolute honour. To top it off, my award made Conference league history because it was the first time all 22 managers had unanimously voted for the same player. The whole experience was very humbling.

During the ceremony, while I'd nipped to the toilet, John Ryan, the Doncaster Rovers chairman, walked in. John, being the vibrant character I now know him to be, introduced himself and sparked a conversation. He congratulated me on my award and said Yeovil had deserved to win the league. I expressed my respect for Doncaster Rovers for winning the play-off final and wished his team luck for the coming season. We both moved up to Division Three (now known as League Two) and we'd soon be up against each other again, or so I thought.

16
Loyalty

I went away on holiday and came back for the start of the 2003/04 pre-season. The media had linked me to a potential move away from Yeovil, with club names like Southampton and Wigan being bandied around. I wanted to speak to GJ about an improved contract because I only had 11 months left on my current one. I felt a rise in salary was justified after such a successful campaign. We'd just won the league, and at the age of 23 I'd won Conference Player of the Year, played 50 games (the most appearances for Yeovil that season), scored 13 goals, and captained the team on numerous occasions. So if that didn't deserve an improved contract, I don't know what did.

I went to see GJ in his office to discuss this. I wasn't asking for millions, I was looking for a small increase in my salary, which was well within their budget. The small increase was a pittance and still equalled a much lower wage than some of the highest-paid players in the Football Conference were earning, bearing in mind that we had now moved up to Division Three.

After speaking with the chairman John Fry, GJ came back and said the club was neither willing to increase my salary nor negotiate. He was very blunt about it. The club had spent hundreds of thousands on a new pitch so

I couldn't understand why they were refusing to negotiate with me. I felt Yeovil had been guilty of this in the past and had lost good players due to their methods of dealing with contract negotiations.

A couple of weeks into pre-season, I was shocked when GJ told me I was no longer to train with the team. Instead I was to train on my own with him every day until further notice. It was clear that GJ and I were no longer seeing eye to eye. My new training session started at 2pm, so instantly disrupted my normal routine. Furthermore, by doing this, GJ definitely upset the balance in the dressing room. It was completely unnecessary. I had to do shuttle runs up and down the pitch, then stand in goal while GJ kicked balls at me, which I was to block without using my hands. So basically he booted balls at my head. The balls he used were the ones players call 'bricks' – balls left to soak in water, making them heavier and rock hard. Every time one pings off your head, it feels like a heavyweight boxer has clumped you one.

After two weeks of this treatment it was clear it was becoming personal. Naturally I was feeling extremely aggrieved. There had been articles in the press casting me as the bad guy and claiming my agent was to blame, but an agent never has any control over this kind of situation. Only a couple of months ago I had been running my balls off to help the team make history, and this was how they treated me?! It really hit a nerve. In football, people talk about loyalty. Fans being loyal to the club. Players being loyal to the club. But rarely is a club's loyalty towards a player mentioned. How can a player be a pivotal part of making club history but then just a short while later be a Judas bastard?

I'd had no thoughts about leaving Yeovil; I'd been the one to approach the club regarding a new contract to stay longer. Nobody in their right mind would want to leave a club they had just been promoted with, unless it was a huge move. The media reports claimed I wanted to leave, but the club's unwillingness to negotiate was conveniently omitted. The only time I really considered leaving was weeks later when GJ asked me to put in a transfer request, which I did. This gave the club the perfect ammunition to make me appear like the bad guy who had no loyalty. When in fact I felt it was the complete fucking opposite.

I found out that Doncaster Rovers had put a bid in to take me up to Yorkshire. It was declined. I appreciate a club doesn't have to tell players when bids go in, however given the circumstances I felt it might have been appropriate. Two days later Doncaster Rovers put a second bid in for me, which again was immediately declined. I lost it. GJ and I had a full-blown argument about how this situation was being handled. Yeovil had refused to negotiate with me and now they were refusing to sell me.

I was beyond angry and decided to pay a visit to the chairman myself, as GJ and I were clearly getting nowhere.

I knocked on John Fry's door, but he wasn't there. I let myself in anyway, sat down in his chair and waited for him. A short spell later he returned to his office to find me behind his desk. Ultimately he was in charge and must have known what was going on. As far as I was aware, he had done nothing to appease the situation so I spoke my mind. He responded by telling me to remove myself from his chair and to sit on the appropriate side of his desk. I did as he asked, allowing him to sit down. He said the reason for declining the two bids from Doncaster Rovers was that they didn't match the club's valuation of me. He told me to wait and see what the forthcoming week would bring. I thanked him for his time and left his office. I took his last comment as a hint that they were dealing with it.

A few days later I received a phone call from GJ, telling me the club had accepted a third and final bid from Doncaster Rovers for £50,000, which still amazes me to this day. Yes, based on the amount they had bought me for, Yeovil had doubled their money, but it was still small change for Division Three. I believe they definitely could have demanded a much higher transfer fee.

Although excited to speak to Doncaster, I felt bitterly disappointed and let down by Yeovil, especially GJ. It was the first time I'd left a club with a sour taste in my mouth.

Before travelling up to Doncaster, I rang Merse to talk it over, just to make sure I wasn't being a dick. He told me I'd shown remarkable patience to put up with such unprofessional behaviour. He understood I was angry but said the best way to channel my emotions was through my performances. I knew he was right and I would try my utmost to show Yeovil what they were missing in the forthcoming season with Rovers.

17
Man-Management

Doncaster Rovers had won the Conference play-off final and moved up into Division Three alongside Yeovil. Having played against them last season, I was already familiar with some of the team. I signed a two-year deal on the pitch at Belle Vue at a pre-season friendly against Rotherham.

I had briefly met the chairman John Ryan at the awards ceremony in Blackpool. Now having met him properly, there was no questioning his evident ambition for the club. John is a very successful businessman and anything he says he's going to do has to be taken seriously. His vision for the club was crystal clear and I loved it.

Location-wise, Doncaster was convenient because it was closer to Edinburgh, so it was easier for my family to travel down to watch me play. Belle Vue was an old football ground with a great atmosphere, where the fans were right on top of you. The last time I'd played there was for Yeovil and we'd thrashed Rovers so I didn't know how the fans were going to take to me. I made my Doncaster debut on 9th August 2003 against Leyton Orient. We won 3-1.

The dressing room culture at Doncaster revolved around drinking, which for obvious reasons didn't sit too well with me. Listening to their drunken stories from the weekend pissed me off because drinking had turned my life upside down. I just didn't want to hear that kind of talk. I'd been sober for almost three years, and since leaving Luton I'd always been the only footballer in the dressing room who didn't drink. At Hereford and Yeovil my teammates had been understanding of my personal battle and I think my teetotal lifestyle had even rubbed off on certain players. Here at Doncaster I found myself preaching because I suspected a couple of the lads might have a similar problem. I even clashed with some of them over it, but I soon realised it was something I was going to have to learn to deal with in my new environment.

My 2003/04 season was shaping up to be better than my last. The chairman told me he'd received offers from other football clubs that wanted to sign me. In the same breath he said he wanted to offer me a three-year contract with an improved wage despite my having signed the two-year deal only three months ago.

Outside training I was still aiming to continually improve my stamina and fitness. I hired a blonde personal trainer, Helen. I'd noticed her in the gym because she had a better six-pack than me! Things became a bit too 'personal' and she became my girlfriend.

I scored my first ever league goal 12 games in, away against Bury, winning 3-1. Two weeks later, I scored my first ever hat trick at home against Bristol Rovers. I knew I was in luck when the last goal rebounded off my arse into the net, winning 5-1.

Then to my astonishment just before my 24th birthday,

I received my first call-up for the Scotland future team in an international friendly against Turkey at Tannadice in Dundee. It was a game to assess fringe players ahead of the 2004 World Cup qualifying campaign. It was a huge step for me. It was only five months ago at Yeovil that Gary Johnson had been firing balls at my head. It was completely out of the blue, and another dream come true.

I came on up front against Turkey after 71 minutes and ran around like a man possessed. We drew 1-1. It was one of the proudest days of my life.

John Ryan asked me for my Scotland shirt. I think, as chairman, he was chuffed that one of his players had been called up, despite playing in Division Three.

True to John's ambition, in that first season at Doncaster we were crowned Division Three champions (now League Two). The previous season in the Conference with Yeovil, we'd finished 17 points above Doncaster; now following my summer move to Doncaster we finished 18 points above Yeovil. How ironic.

I went on to win the PFA Division Three Player of the Year. For me, to win the highest individual accolade again was an unbelievable achievement. I was also the only Doncaster player to be named in the PFA Team of the Year, even though the team won the league! My success had a lot to do with my lifestyle, good mentoring from Merse, and the dietary advice Matthew Upson shared with me while he was in the England squad under Sven-Göran Eriksson. Another major component, though, was my left back Tim Ryan. Being a hard tackler and extremely vocal made him a dream to work with. Some full backs spend the whole game calling you back to help them because they shit themselves in one-vs-one situations, but Tim was the polar opposite. If I ever came back into my own half he would go mad at me. He wasn't the quickest, but as soon as he got the ball his first thought was to find me. He would scream at me to attack the opposition full back, which for me, as a winger, was music to my ears.

When the season finished John offered me another brand-new three-year contract. He said, "Michael, that's how we do business here. You play well, you get rewarded."

I was very blessed and lucky to have a chairman who was so appreciative of my work. John Ryan absolutely loved Doncaster. He had a lot of history and affiliation with the town. Most chairmen only care about financial gain, but this was John's boyhood team and the club meant so much more to him. His brother Phil was the photographer on match days and he would always have a pleasant word to say to me before a game.

The team celebrated the win at Doncaster Town Hall. I stepped onto the Mayor's balcony holding the trophy with John and my girlfriend Helen, looking out on thousands of Doncaster Rovers fans. When the crowd cheered at the sight of us holding the trophy, Helen's face turned bright red. It was a special moment for all of us, even Helen, who was a local lass and had never experienced anything like that before.

It was a relief to finally be back in League One, where I'd started with Luton Town. This time I was fitter and more experienced. I knew the new 2004/05 season would be tougher but I couldn't wait to attack it.

During a discussion with the club doctor about the health benefits of not drinking alcohol over the last five years, he said my body had probably fully repaired itself from the damage I'd caused. I'd focussed all my efforts on being an athlete and maintaining my 7% body fat.

We had a few players who were slightly below the standard we needed, so the chairman brought in a couple of new signings to try and strengthen the squad. John Ryan used to call me most Saturdays after a match to talk it through. He would also invite me over to Cheshire to talk football. He was always happy and is an extremely positive person. He had a beautiful home and a lovely family. He even had a full-size football pitch in his garden where we used to have penalty shoot-outs. He'd bombard me with questions on penalty-taking. How could I tell which way the keeper would dive? How did I know which corner to kick the ball into? It was a unique bond between player and chairman.

We had a Yorkshire derby against Barnsley, away at Oakwell, on a foggy Wednesday night. We beat them 3-1. In the dressing room before the match, I recall the manager Dave Penney saying openly to our centre midfielders that all of Barnsley's play went through Stephen McPhail and to make sure someone left one on him as soon as possible. To me it was pretty clear what that meant. Six minutes into the game, Stephen McPhail was stretchered off with medial knee ligament damage, putting him out of action for a couple of months.

Professional players know when a tackle against them is malicious. Although local derbies are always fiercely contested, I believe the Barnsley players felt very aggrieved after this tackle was made. There was a real bitterness between both sets of players and over the next three games, five red cards and five yellow cards were shown.

Over time I'd come to the conclusion that I really didn't like Dave Penney. In my opinion his lack of experience as a manager had started to show.

We had a midweek match against Bradford City at home on 24th March 2005. I was just about to leave my house when the doorbell rang. I remember it vividly. I was surprised to see Mickey Walker (our coach) and Baz Richardson (our goalkeeping coach) on my doorstep. It was two hours before kick-off. I thought maybe the match had been cancelled.

They were there to pass on the message from Dave that I was not to turn up to the match that night. Both men looked apologetic and couldn't give me an answer as to why. I honestly thought they were joking. I got in the car and drove to the ground. On the way I called my agent. He couldn't shine much light on the situation, but did suggest it might be due to the fact that other scouts or managers could be coming to watch me play as it was a Thursday night and there were no other fixtures on.

I was always in the starting line-up, I'd been scoring goals, I wasn't playing poorly and my form was good, plus things were fine off the pitch too. So why the fuck was I being told not to show up? It didn't make any sense to me. We were only a few points from the play-offs.

I pulled up to the ground at the same time as the chairman. John could see I was angry and asked me what was going on. I told him what Mickey and Baz had just said. John was genuinely shocked and told me he'd speak to Dave. He looked pissed off.

I went straight to the dressing room to wait until Dave turned up to pick the team. As he entered he looked shocked to see me there. He stuttered as he told me I wasn't in the squad and asked me to wait in his office. Dave started to select the team for the match. I didn't want to cause a scene in front of the players; it was a big game for us. So after hearing the starting line-up I sat in his office as I didn't want the lads to lose focus. I could tell they were as confused as I was by the situation.

Mickey and Baz were already in there. I had always respected Mickey's opinion, he's a great coach and I thought he was a top bloke. For all the shouting I was doing, I knew my issue wasn't with him – it was strictly with Dave. Mickey said he thought it was transfer speculation that was causing the issue, which is what my agent suspected too. I didn't care what it was; I should have been playing. Two minutes later Dave walked in, so Mickey and Baz walked out to avoid the imminent argument.

I challenged him immediately and pointed out what Mickey and my agent had said about transfer speculation. It didn't make any sense that just because other managers might be watching me, he was willing to drop me, possibly risking the team's success. We needed the three points. Dave told me he didn't think my head was on the game and that I was too into my football. What the fuck did that even mean? Yes, I am an intense player. Yes, I lived football. I want to watch every game when I go home. I want to study my next opponent's strengths and weaknesses before the upcoming match. I think Dave just liked football, and I always thought he was a bit put out that John and I got on so well. With nothing left to say, I walked out. I was fucking livid.

Frustrated, I went upstairs to the boardroom to find John. He calmed me down and told me to go and watch the match from the director's seats. He would speak to Dave tomorrow. I knew our focus must be on the game in hand.

There were a few managers there from Championship and Premiership clubs including Neil Warnock from Sheffield United. As he sat down in front of me he said, "Every time I come to watch you play, son, he never picks you."

It struck such a chord with me. All players get dropped at some point, but never told to stay at home and not come to the match. I sat there thinking to myself that this could have been the game that got us even closer to the play-offs, or put me back in the Scotland squad, or impressed another manager. Every game is a shop window. I was so angry because my form was good and whatever this was, it wasn't performance related.

At half-time supporters asked me why I wasn't playing and if I was injured. I just told them the truth – that I was fully fit and my absence was purely down to the manager's decision. The game finished 1-1.

Four days later we played Tranmere away. Surprise, surprise, I was back in the team. I scored after just three minutes. All the lads jumped on me. Greg Blundell whispered in my ear, "Best way to show him, Macca!"

We won 4-2.

In the 2004/05 campaign we had a respectable season, finishing 10th in League One. I made 51 appearances and scored 12 goals.

Matthew Upson called me for a chat just before boarding a plane with the England squad. He asked me, "How the fuck has your ugly mug been chosen as one of the five footballers of the year when you're not even in the Premier League?"

It turned out he'd picked up The Times Football Yearbook 2004-05 at the airport and there I was alongside Steven Gerrard, Thierry Henry, Frank Lampard and Wayne Rooney. I couldn't help but agree with him that it was a shock. But only after I'd reminded him that his name wasn't mentioned!

Off the pitch, Helen had noticed a house on a new development in Doncaster near to the stadium and training ground. I felt settled with her so decided to buy it. I also hadn't forgotten the promise I'd made to my mum when I left the estate, so I bought another house in the Silverknowles area of Edinburgh that she liked. It had just been built so Helen and I drove up to fully furnish the house for her before she moved in. I wanted everything to be brand new and perfect. Mum was so overwhelmed when she opened the front door that she burst into tears. It was the first time in her life that she'd had a real place to call home.

I felt proud that I was now in a financial position to do this for my mum. People measure success in different ways but getting out of a drug-dealing gang life, overcoming alcohol addiction, playing for my country and now being able to look after my mum, for me equalled success.

18
Underdog

We started the new 2005/06 season off well but our Carling Cup run was to be our highlight. In the first round we beat Wrexham 1-0. In the second round we were up against Manchester City at home. I was excited. This was a good time for me to test my ability against Premiership opposition.

The Man City game went to extra time with Darius Vassell opening the scoring. However thanks to Ben Thatcher taking Lewis Guy down in the box, I scored an equalising penalty in the dying minutes of extra time against David James, bringing the score level and taking it into penalties.

Both teams stood on the halfway line after Stuart Pearce and Dave Penney had selected their team's top five penalty takers. I always asked to go first because I spent a lot of time with goalkeepers practising penalty kicks. I also used to go in goal so I could understand what the keepers could see in a player's body language on the run-up to approach the ball.

The problem with a penalty shoot-out is you have a lot more time on the lonely walk up to the penalty spot to consider where the hell you're going to stick the ball. I'd just slotted one past David James keeping us in the competition and now, just a few minutes later, I found myself staring him down again. That's where the mind games begin. I know he's thinking what I'm thinking. Am I going to stick the ball in the same place or put it in the opposite corner?

I went through my usual routine of taking the ball with both hands and kissing it, with a quick prayer to the big man upstairs. I always try to block out any noise and any doubt. I focus on my contact with the ball. I put it onto the penalty spot but I never make a decision about which direction I might go in until I have walked back for my run-up. I do this because as soon as you put the ball down, goalkeepers automatically start analysing your body position and angle to see if there's any suggestion as to which way you might go. People used to talk about eye contact. But your eyes don't kick the football. The biggest giveaway is in that split second before you make contact – it's your standing foot and your arms, the key components for balance, which the best keepers are trained to study.

 Luckily for me and the team, I won the mind game putting us 1-0 up in the shoot-out. Our substitute keeper Jan Budtz was to be the hero, saving two penalties from Antoine Sibierski and Richard Dunne. We won 3-0 on penalties, putting us through to the next round.

Our winning streak continued after beating Gillingham 2-0 in the third round.

In the fourth round we turned over Aston Villa at Belle Vue winning 3-0. I put Rovers in the lead, 20 minutes in after scoring a penalty when Villa's Liam Ridgewell handled the ball in the box. I slotted the ball straight into the corner of the net. Paul Heffernan side-footed our next goal in, making it 2-0. Then with 12 minutes to go Sean Thornton shot from outside the box, which was deflected in, for our third and final goal. The fans went mad. We looked more like the Premiership side that night. Sky gave me the Man of the Match award – and for any player performing live on TV, this always puts your stock up a little.

We were now through to the quarter-finals against Arsenal. A few hours before the match, I was going through my usual pre-match routine, enjoying a bowl of pasta with my feet up. My phone rang. It was the chairman, John Ryan. He had something important to ask me. He wanted my opinion on how the rest of the team would feel if he sacked Dave Penney before the game. I told him I didn't think they would care as many of them, including myself, didn't like him. There was also the fact that John was the one who paid our wages. I was curious about who he had in mind to take charge if he went ahead with his decision. He told me that he would lead the team talk and that Mickey Walker would take the match.

After a five-minute conversation we came to the conclusion that Dave Penney should keep his job. We were only three points off the play-offs and playing Arsenal live on Sky in just a few hours' time. It probably wasn't the best timing!

On paper Dave Penney had just achieved back-to-back promotions from Conference to League One. We'd finished 10th the previous season, and at that time we were in the quarter-final of the Carling Cup. That said, there's a certain way to treat people who do well for you, and in my opinion Dave rubbed many people up the wrong way. Now I knew that the writing was on the wall for him.

It was the first time I'd ever been asked my thoughts on whether or not a manager should be sacked from the hierarchy. It showed how much John trusted my opinion.

The atmosphere during night matches at Belle Vue was incredible and that night was no different. I imagine Arsenal's arrival at our changing facilities was a bit of a culture shock for them. The opposition changing rooms were probably a fifth of the size of a Premiership dressing room, so by the time a 20-man squad had squeezed in, they would have been cramped and uncomfortable. Plus only one shower worked. I know all these things don't sound like much, but they really piss players off.

Four minutes into the game I knocked the ball past Philippe Senderos and sneaked one in off the near post, beating keeper Manuel Almunia from an almost impossible angle, putting us 1-0 up.

Arsenal's Robin van Persie came off after 33 minutes injured, which spurred us on even more.

Not long into the second half Quincy Owusu-Abeyie scored, making it 1-1. With the game level we went into extra time. On the 104th minute I crossed the ball into the box and after a mix-up in Arsenal's defence, Paul Green put us back into the lead. It looked like we were going to go through to the semi-final until Arsenal's captain

Gilberto Silva got on the end of a cross from Emmanuel Eboué, scoring a late equaliser with a minute to go, forcing a penalty shoot-out. When his goal hit the back of the net I felt the deflation sweep through the stadium. It was cruel. We had held on for so long.

I stepped up to take the first penalty and scored. Neil Roberts hit the post and both Paul Heffernan and Paul Green's penalties were saved, leaving us to ponder what might have been. We lost 3-1 on penalties and Arsenal went on to play Wigan Athletic in the semi-finals, who surprisingly beat them. Wigan faced Manchester United in the final, losing 4-0.

In the tunnel I swapped shirts with Gilberto Silva. Out of appreciation for the effort we'd put in, he also gave me his captain's armband, which was a lovely touch. I think we'd given them a tougher time than they were expecting.

Even though everyone praised us for getting that far in the competition, I was bitterly disappointed. I'd wanted to win. I felt we'd done enough to put Arsenal to bed. I always look to demand more of myself and of those around me. If something has the potential to be great, why accept good or average? I believe in consistently trying to break the boundaries of expectation and ambition. I'm single-minded and in football if you take your eye off the prize for a split second, it will bite you on the arse. Not all footballers are like this. Some are just sheep, bleating in agreement with whatever they're told, even if deep down they know it's wrong. Then others are actually more scared of success than failure because it takes them too far out of their comfort zone.

I never washed Gilberto Silva's shirt because it still had the grass stain on it from where he'd slid to score that late equalising goal. It was a constant reminder to me of how fine the line is between success and failure.

***

In my opinion it's unlikely that any current League One team will ever lift the League Cup or FA Cup. It's unfair that higher division teams are allowed to come in at the later stages of the competition. Lower league teams spend hours thrashing it out in the first couple of rounds and have probably picked up some injuries along the way. Doncaster Rovers, along with many other 'underdog' teams, have proved it is possible to beat Premiership clubs. So why shouldn't these clubs start in round one with the rest of us?

Take the FA Cup, for example; Premiership and Championship teams enter the competition at the third round, after most non-league and league teams have played numerous games. Teams in the lower leagues have smaller squads and, in theory, less quality players. On top of that, most league teams play 46 matches per season compared to the Premiership who play only 38.

I appreciate that the top six Premiership teams qualify for the Champions League and UEFA Europa League, but what about the other 14 Premiership teams? They play in exactly the same competitions but have no European commitments. I agree that the non-league qualifiers should go ahead. But the competition would be fairer and more financially beneficial, particularly to grass-root sides, if all teams (even if it were only the other 14 Premiership teams) were to start in round one! Ensure the matches have a winner or loser on the day with a penalty shoot-out. The loser is knocked out and you have a much fairer competition.

***

By Christmas we were still in the top ten. However I think we'd put so much effort into the Carling Cup games that we'd let our league performances dwindle. We only won one out of our next eight games.

I received a call from an old Luton teammate who's well respected in the game. He said my agent hadn't been doing his job properly. He told me Premiership and Championship managers had been trying to contact my agent about me but he'd failed to return their calls. I didn't know why my agent would do this when he knew I wanted to play at a higher level.

My mate would never lie to me, especially about something like this, so I took what he said on board. Playing in League One wouldn't help my chances of being selected for the Scotland team so my agent obviously had to go.

I knew if I didn't act immediately I might miss another opportunity. So I invited him round one night to talk but I didn't tell him about the phone call I'd received. When he arrived I locked the door behind him. I asked him what the fuck was going on. I knew by his reaction something wasn't right. In my very polite Scottish way, I asked him to sign a pre-prepared document, releasing me from my contractual obligations with the agency he worked for. He signed it quickly and left my house.

I found a new agent, the well-respected Hayden Evans from HN Sports in Leeds, and we understood each other from the get-go.

Off the back of the Carling Cup run, I'd had some good publicity. In December I'd won League One Player of the Month. My relationship with Dave Penney was still strained, to say the least. He'd put me on the bench for four consecutive matches when I'd been playing well and already scored 13 goals from midfield. One afternoon Dave called me into his office to inform me that Sheffield Wednesday who were in the Championship had asked to take me on loan until the end of the season. But he wasn't going to allow it. Instead of having a full-blown row with Dave, I ranted at my new agent Hayden about speaking to this fucking geezer.

Dave wasn't selecting me for Doncaster, nor was he allowing me to showcase my talent at Sheffield Wednesday in a higher division. As always with Dave, his problem with me was personal not football related. If in the unlikely event he ever got to manage in the Premier League, I always wondered how the fuck he would cope with more opinionated players than me who had double the ego? I know I can come across as an arrogant fucker, but my professionalism since leaving Luton Town had been unquestionable and my performances had more often than not spoken for themselves. I become very angry when I feel my career progression is being hindered.

Hayden spoke with the manager and the chairman to tell them something had to give. He didn't want one of his players, who should have been starting regularly, sitting on the bench when it was obvious that other clubs from higher divisions were interested in him. Dave still wouldn't budge.

The following week Matthew Upson called me. One of his friends Terry Westley had been given the caretaker manager's job at Derby County and asked if I thought Doncaster would let me go on loan until the end of the season? I laughed and told him how Dave had just knocked back a loan move to Sheffield Wednesday. I told him I would speak to John Ryan to see if he would intervene, as I didn't trust leaving the situation in Dave's hands.

I talked it through with John and he gave me permission to go to Derby and that both Secretaries would discuss the finer details in the morning. He had always promised me he would never stand in the way of my career. After all, it was only a loan move for a few months and I still had over a year left on my current contract with Doncaster.

Hayden called Derby. They wanted me down there that night. The hotel was booked and I was to be at the training ground for 9am. Helen wasn't overly impressed at my speedy departure but that's the nature of the business.

In the morning Hayden and I drove to Derby's training ground. I couldn't help but be instantly impressed by the facilities. I met with Terry Westley and all the necessary paperwork was taken care of. He said it was imperative Derby remained in the Championship as they were teetering too close to the relegation zone. He wanted to thank Dave Penney so decided to give him a quick call. I could hear the conversation unfold. I heard Dave splutter when Terry said he was sitting opposite me. He clearly had no idea what was going on. Terry told Dave to check with the Doncaster chairman. He put the phone down and laughed. We shook hands and Terry said he'd see me in the morning for training.

As we started to pull away from the training ground, one of the coaching staff came running over to the car shouting and waving his arms to stop us from leaving. There was a complication. I went back inside to speak to Terry again to find out exactly what was happening. Terry explained that Dave wanted a Derby player in exchange for me. That wasn't the deal. I made a call to John Ryan, who was fuming with Dave by the end of it. He told me to assure Terry that everything we'd agreed would go ahead.

True to John's word, the deal went through. I now had two months to help keep Derby County in the Championship.

19
The Penney Dropped

Derby County was my first taste of Championship football. Described as one of the hardest leagues in football, I relished the unpredictability of it. Despite it being only a two-month loan deal, I felt it was a fantastic opportunity. I knew I needed to work hard and make an impact to secure a deal in the summer with Derby or another Championship club. I didn't want to go back to Doncaster while Dave Penney was still the manager.

On Saturday 11th March 2006, I made my debut for Derby against Burnley at home, winning 3-0. After coming out of the Premier League a few seasons earlier, Derby's infrastructure was more than ready to go back to the top flight. Although in my opinion, they definitely needed a few more players to help them achieve this. One of the things that impressed me the most was the vast number of back-room staff the club employed to look after the players.

Within a matter of days of putting on a Derby County shirt I received my second international call-up. Scotland had appointed Rangers' legends Walter Smith and Ally McCoist as the new manager and coach. It's always an honour to be called up for your country but to be called up by these two was extra special. I know one side of my family were extremely pleased. I'd grown up watching Super Ally playing for Rangers against Hearts when they came to the capital.

Once again the international friendly was against Turkey, but this time in Inverness. I was in the starting line-up. We lost 3-2 but it gave me more valuable insight to the standard of international football. Before heading back down to Derby I had a quick chat with Ally as we got off the coach at Hampden Park. He told me next season it was essential I was competing in the Championship or Premier League to keep my name in the hat for selection. It was a valid point which I took note of.

I went on to play eight out of the remaining nine games for Derby County that season finishing 20th, 12 points clear of relegation. Terry's objective had been achieved. I'd been used to fighting for promotions but I felt that, given the circumstances, I'd played a small part in keeping the club in the Championship. Millwall, Crewe and Brighton were eventually relegated.

Derby would be looking to appoint a new manager in the summer. Terry pulled me aside and told me if he was awarded the job there would be a contract there for me but not to hold my breath, as he didn't think it would be him who got it. In June 2006, Derby appointed Billy Davies so I returned to Doncaster Rovers.

During the summer, while I was away in the south of Spain with Helen, Barnsley played Swansea City in the League One play-off final. Hayden rang me before the game to say whoever won the match and was promoted to the Championship was probably the team I'd be playing for next season. Hayden had always been reliable. A lot of players were never clear on what they wanted to achieve from their time at a club. We had a strategy and stuck to it. It's so important to have trust and understanding between player and agent. Hayden looked after many experienced big names from the Premiership who had been with him their whole careers. I considered myself to be in good hands, so if he said I was going to play for whichever team won the play-off final that day, I believed him.

I was hoping it would be Swansea City because there was still a lot of ill feeling towards me from the Barnsley players due to previous Yorkshire derbies being a bit tasty. It was a strange feeling watching the final with Helen, asking myself which one would be best for me. Both were good clubs. Swansea City would probably pay more but Helen wanted Barnsley to win. Being from Yorkshire, she wanted to stay close to her family and friends. The game went into penalties and Barnsley won 4-3. Helen was delighted.

After my summer break I went back to Doncaster for pre-season training where Dave, of course, had a lovely warm welcome for me. A few days in, John Ryan called to tell me he'd accepted an offer from newly-promoted Championship side Barnsley for £125,000. I was grateful to John for not standing in my way of playing Championship football – although I was disappointed that I never got to play at the new stadium in a Rovers shirt. Despite the issues I'd had with Dave, I'd had a great time at Doncaster and had a close affiliation with the supporters.

One month later, I wasn't shocked at all when the news was announced that Dave Penney was no longer the Doncaster Rovers manager.

20
Negotiator

Following Barnsley FC's promotion from League One the previous season, I knew there would be a positive vibe around the club. The manager was ex-Leeds United player Andy Ritchie. His team had done tremendously well to reach the play-off final and win. If I signed for Barnsley I was fully aware that the forthcoming campaign wouldn't be easy because the club didn't have many experienced Championship players.

Prior to meeting the chairman and manager at Oakwell, Hayden and I discussed what I wanted in terms of personal wages and length of contract. I was expecting a better offer from Barnsley than their initial proposition. I wasn't pleased with the financial package on the table, as it gave only a slight increase on my current contract at Doncaster. I mentioned to Hayden there was a possibility the deal might fall through. However, following feedback from inside sources, it became apparent that Barnsley didn't have a massive budget to play with. What they were offering was about right for the club at the time.

This is where Hayden comes into his own. He's a very shrewd negotiator. He told the club I would sign a two-year contract but only on the condition that Barnsley included a clause stating that if another club wanted to buy me at end of the season with an offer in excess of £125,000, I could leave immediately. This was obviously a starting point for us. We were expecting Barnsley to respond with a figure of around £250,000-£500,000.

To Hayden's surprise and mine, they agreed to £125,000. This meant they'd agreed a fixed selling fee after 12 months – and for the same price as they'd literally just paid for me. Hayden knew that if I maintained the form I'd been displaying in the coming season, based on this clause other Championship clubs would be hovering like vultures. I quickly put pen to paper and signed the contract. I was happy, Hayden was happy, and Barnsley had a new left winger.

When I first walked into my new dressing room, only half the players bothered to shake my hand. Many of them still held a grudge from past encounters when I had been at Doncaster. This isn't uncommon in football. I knew it would take some time so I didn't let it distract my focus from why I was there.

I moved house to Badsworth, just outside Barnsley. Helen couldn't understand why we were bothering to move only 30 minutes away, whereas I knew that the Doncaster faithful would probably be pissed off at me for signing with a Yorkshire rival.

I made my Barnsley debut at home to Cardiff, losing 2-1 on 5th August 2006. This was the first time in my career that my opening match had resulted in a loss. As time went on, I started to get to know the lads and they eventually warmed to me. The Championship suited my style of play and I scored five goals in my first 18 games with help from full back Paul Heckingbottom.

Helen and Hayden came to watch me play in a Yorkshire derby against Leeds United at home. Hayden is a passionate Leeds fan. In the 62nd minute I hit a low shot from just outside the 18-yard box which arrowed into the bottom corner of the net. The fans went bananas and I ran over to the corner flag where I knew Hayden was sitting with Helen. While I was celebrating I pointed up to Hayden knowing he would be riled that I'd scored against his team. He was laughing but I could tell he didn't know whether to throw something at me or clap. We won 3-2.

***

Usually I would leave the football ground at around 1pm every day, so I had loads of free time after training. I used my afternoons to look at residential property and learn from people I personally knew in the industry. Sometimes I would help my teammates identify properties to buy. I was trying to build a small portfolio myself for when I retired, so I decided to buy a flat in Doncaster to add to what I already owned. I also set up a small valeting business, which Helen's brother ran for me, because I knew footballers spent a fortune having their cars cleaned. I realised it wasn't going to be a big money-spinner but it kept Helen's brother busy and taught me a bit more about running my own small business. I was halfway through my career and had begun to think about life after football.

One of my dreams has always been to set up a business and make it hugely successful.

***

Barnsley were in the bottom half, fluttering in and out of the relegation zone. The team were so unfit and unfocussed. As far as I was concerned the players got away with murder. Some days the lads would arrive late to training, hungover, carrying a McDonald's breakfast. It was so unprofessional. We were supposed to be athletes. The manager worked on the basis that he trusted the players and this style had got them promoted, but having witnessed the standard at Derby County I knew that some of these players were definitely not equipped to play at Championship level. I'd been at Barnsley for just over three months and felt the dressing room lacked winners. I don't mind being in a dog fight as long as everyone else is giving their all, but I just didn't feel that was the case here. A month later, Andy Ritchie was sacked. The board appointed Simon Davey from Barnsley's Youth Academy as caretaker manager. It was a turbulent week for the football club.

The new manager called a meeting with all the players for the following morning, but I'd heard on the grapevine that Wolverhampton Wanderers had put a bid in for me – a move I was certainly interested in pursuing. In my opinion Barnsley were going to be in a relegation battle all season and the bottom line was I wanted to get into the Premier League. I needed to act quickly, though, as the transfer window closed at 5pm the next day. I rang the Barnsley chairman Gordon Shepherd to confirm the bid and arranged to meet him in the morning to discuss my future at the club. He said the bid had been rejected but he was willing to meet me at 10am.

Hayden couldn't make the morning meeting as he was away, but he told me the HN Sports team were on standby. I felt confident enough to handle it on my own. Hayden wouldn't normally recommend that a player negotiate such situations, but time was of the essence. I decided to wear a suit, rather than my usual tracksuit, and drove to the training ground early the next day. I bumped into the new gaffer as I walked in. We hadn't met properly before so I introduced myself and explained I would have to miss his team meeting due to my appointment with the chairman.

I ran into a few of the players in the corridor, who seeing my unusual attire questioned me. I told them the situation. They shook my hand and wished me luck. It was funny because only a few months previously, half of them wouldn't even shake my hand, but now I felt they didn't want to see me go! It's funny how relationships can be so fickle in football.

I believed I'd be more likely to gain a promotion at Wolves than at Barnsley. Having played with the team for almost four months, I didn't believe they were good enough, compared to other Championship teams, to get me to where I wanted to be. That may sound selfish but this was my career and I was going to do whatever it took to achieve my dreams.

I sat outside the chairman Gordon Shepherd's office for at least a couple of hours, then at around midday he sauntered in. I held my tongue despite being irritated that he'd kept me waiting so long. The transfer deadline closed at 5pm and this was now going to be ridiculously tight. I cut to the chase.

Gordon said they'd rejected a second offer from Wolves that morning, as it was way off his valuation. I had to remind him of the £125,000 transfer clause stated in my contract. He said it didn't really matter as it only became applicable after the end of the season. Barnsley were second from the bottom in the league and I made it clear a relegation battle would not help my chances of making the Scottish national team again. There was a lot of chat and time was passing by. I was becoming frustrated because I had the feeling he was wasting time on purpose.

For me it's all about career progression and as he wasn't going to let me go to Wolves, I decided there and then that enough was enough. He clearly wasn't going to budge so I called his bluff and told him I'd fuck off on holiday then. He stared at me in sheer surprise and I could tell by his face he wasn't sure if I was being serious or not.

Was I bluffing? No. I lived for football but this was a negotiation and Hayden would have been giving the chairman a much tougher time of it. Hayden had taught me well and I was trying to put myself in a stronger position because I understood that the chairman held all the cards and dictated the final say. I was just letting him know what

I would consider doing. I know that 95% of footballers wouldn't even have been in that room, let alone having that conversation. My boldness probably comes from my upbringing. I don't believe a man's title or job should mean I can't speak my mind to him.

The room fell silent for a moment as we locked horns. It was now or never. Then Gordon's secretary buzzed to say he had a phone call, which he took outside. When he returned he said Wolves had put a final offer in, one he had accepted. As he stood up to shake my hand, he told me to come back and see him when I finished playing football because he'd have a job for me.

I had under an hour to agree my salary with Wolves and for the paperwork to reach the FA.

Next I spoke to Jez Moxey, chief executive at Wolves. I told him I wanted Wolves to at least try to double my current salary, which would be a low wage based on what I'd heard other Wolves players were on. I was prepared to sign a contract for two and a half years on the proviso that at the end of the current season, as long as I did well for the club, I would be expecting him to offer me an improved contract.

Jez Moxey assured me that if I performed well for the club, an improved contract would be delivered at the end of the season.

With no time to make any changes, all I could hear was John Moore's voice in my head telling me to get the pissing contract signed, sonny, and worry about the rest later.

I waited nervously for confirmation from the FA that the deal had gone through. A few minutes later they confirmed they'd received it with just two minutes to spare.

21
Wandering Star

Wolves had a match against Sunderland that Friday. The manager Mick McCarthy thought it would be a good idea for me to meet the staff and the players then.

Before that evening's game, Wolves were sitting 10th in the Championship. I took Helen with me to Molineux. We met the football liaison officer who showed us to the manager's office. The coaching staff and Mick McCarthy were all there, tucking into some pre-match sandwiches. After some introductions they invited us both to join them. Usually the WAGs remain upstairs so it made a nice change for Helen.

I remember the game as if it was yesterday due to the media frenzy that surrounded the match. It was the first time Mick McCarthy and Roy Keane had gone head to head with their respective teams since the World Cup saga in Saipan. The Sunderland team arrived and I saw Roy Keane walking down the corridor towards the manager's office. As Mick opened the door I remember thinking that this was going to be interesting!

It was extremely brief and when Mick returned to his office, he cracked a joke about it. Not long after, he took me to meet the players in the dressing room. Unlike my first day at Barnsley, though, I actually got a handshake from everyone.

I left feeling positive about my new teammates. I met Helen again and we were escorted to the director's box to watch the match. The game finished in a draw.

I made my debut for Wolves in a 1-1 draw against Crystal Palace at home on Tuesday 28th November 2006.

Wolves had an experienced team and quite a few international players. I'd linked up well with Jay Bothroyd, and the team was creeping up the table. I firmly believed that the club would be back in the Premier League in the next few seasons. However the squad was huge, which was a waste of money, especially when half of them weren't even playing or were always injured.

I bought a lovely big house in Perton for just under £1 million. What I didn't know was that Mick McCarthy had been looking at the same house. Probably not the best way to get on your new gaffer's good side!

I scored my first goal for Wolves against Sheffield Wednesday, heading the ball home in the 35th minute after a great cross from Michael Kightly. We drew again, 2-2.

With three games to go, we were 6th and trying to secure a play-off spot. I'd been working all week with Terry Connor, the coach, on attacking the ball in the air from crosses. We had an early kick-off that Sunday against Birmingham City in the West Midlands derby. That day the atmosphere at Molineux was electric. Police were everywhere, reminding me it was probably a Category C+ game, which means there's an increased risk of trouble between rival fans. It was like being back in Edinburgh for a Hearts vs Hibs derby. My favourite memory from Wolves is walking through the Jack Harris stand from the players' car park; it gave me a sense of being a fan again before kick-off.

It was 0-0 at half-time, but the second half sprang into life when Blues' Andy Cole looped one over our oncoming goalkeeper Matt Murray from a tight angle. I brought us back level when Michael Kightly beat the full back and stood up a cross to the back post, and I headed the ball downwards into the net. Then just a few minutes later, I scored another header inside the six-yard box, outjumping Bruno N'Gotty from a lovely flighted Andy Keogh cross, putting us ahead. Then Nicklas Bendtner scored a bullet of a header to bring the score level again, 2-2. With the clock ticking, Cameron Jerome beat the offside trap and ran into the box, side-footing Birmingham into the lead.

The referee awarded Wolves a free kick in injury time. There were only minutes left, so I whipped the ball into the box. To the entire stadium's amazement the referee pointed to the penalty spot, after a dubious foul on Jody Craddock. I knew this would be the last kick of the game.

I grabbed the ball, confident I could make it 3-3 and complete my hat trick. The previous season I think I'd scored more penalties than any other player in the English leagues. A bit too overconfidently I side-footed the softest penalty ever, which was saved. I was fucking raging at myself. I should have just smashed it as hard as I could. It still angers me now, just thinking about it.

I had to take it on the chin, and I apologised to the fans through the media. I have no shame in admitting when I've fucked up, as I certainly don't hold back when I know I've done a good job.

Luckily for me, it didn't change our position in the league and we won our last two games finishing 5th, securing a play-off position. We went on to play West Bromwich Albion in the semi-finals.

In the first leg at Molineux, West Brom beat us 3-2. In the second leg at the Hawthorns, the game was very tight. We only needed one goal to get us back in it. After 59 minutes Mick McCarthy took me off and put a defensive midfielder on. Incensed, I kicked a chair in the dugout and had a few choice words with him. Six minutes later Kevin Phillips scored, putting any chance of a comeback to bed. This was my 52nd game of the season; I'd scored eight goals and had 14 assists. I could not for the life of me understand his logic in taking me off the pitch. To me, it showed a complete lack of belief in my ability as a player.

After the match I couldn't hold back and I had a few more choice words with the manager, sparking an argument. He did apologise for taking me off, but the season was over.

I returned for pre-season training in July 2007 with one clear aim in mind; I wanted to hold Jez Moxey to his word about my contract. Although I still had two years left on my current deal, he'd agreed back on 22nd November 2006 that if I did well on the pitch he'd increase my salary. I went to see Jez at the training ground. After a brief discussion he informed me he would only talk to me about an increase in my salary six months from now. I reminded him of the conversation we'd had on transfer deadline day. I knew he was trying to palm me off. I was infuriated. The bottom line was, since signing for Wolves halfway through the season I'd played every game. When I joined we were 10th and yet we'd finished 5th, losing to West Brom in the play-off semi-finals.

Only the Wolverhampton Wanderers' faithful, who travel up and down the country every week to watch their team play, can judge whether Jez Moxey was fair or not.

22
Reunited

Not long into pre-season and after Jez's dismissive comments about my contract, Mick McCarthy told me they'd received an offer from Bristol City. When I asked him to give me 24 hours to think about it, he was surprised I was willing to even contemplate it, knowing that Gary Johnson and I weren't on the best terms. I called my former teammate Lee Johnson to try to find out if GJ was fully behind the bid. Without saying too much, he assured me that if Wolves gave me permission to go down to Bristol for contract talks, his dad and I were likely to come to an agreement. It had been four years since GJ had kicked balls at my head. He'd always been a great manager and knew how to get the best out of me, but I wasn't sure we could put it behind us.

I went in the following morning to see Mick. I told him I would like to speak to Bristol City to see what they were offering. He looked a bit pissed off but gave me permission anyway. We finished the conversation with a strong handshake. Although he's not my favourite manager, I respect Mick McCarthy a great deal for what he's achieved in football as a player and as a manager.

Wolves accepted a bid for me from Bristol City of around £450,000.

***

I wasn't apprehensive about going down to Bristol but I did take a moment to reflect on my life. I had properties. I had beautiful cars on the drive. My signature was now worth millions. I was selfishly living my dream, but at what cost? All the moving around had taken its toll on my relationship with Helen. Every time she started to settle into a new home, we'd move again – and now a potential transfer to Bristol meant she'd be even further away from her family. That summer, after five good years, we parted. She moved into the flat in Doncaster, taking with her our English mastiff Diego. I felt lost. Helen's understanding of the industry and the effort she'd put into our relationship had definitely helped me to focus solely on football. I regret not having invested the same level of effort as she did. I'd been ridiculously selfish and self-centred.

***

I hadn't spoken to GJ properly since my final days at Yeovil Town. Things had ended on a bitter note so we needed to clear the air before we could move forward. I didn't hold a grudge but I'm also not the type of person to brush things under the carpet. I still had huge respect for GJ, no matter how things had been left. I drove to Bristol to have a discussion with him. He openly admitted that he regretted how he'd handled the previous situation. I was grateful that he'd acknowledged his part in it all. GJ asked me to put my property interests on hold and to concentrate entirely on football, which I agreed to do. I thought he'd shown a big pair of balls in wanting to work with me again. We now had the opportunity to put it all behind us and attempt to get Bristol City into the Premier League.

That week I signed a three-year deal with Bristol City. I was happy knowing that GJ had always given me the freedom to express myself on the pitch; he understood my manic drive and passion for the game.

Coming up from League One, GJ was on the hunt for players who he felt could perform in the Championship. He signed Lee Trundle from Swansea City, Marvin Elliott from Millwall, Ivan Sproule from Hibs and Darren Byfield on a free transfer.

GJ had done a remarkable job in getting the team promoted, especially considering that last year three of his first team players had been sent to prison after a brawl. In the previous four seasons GJ had achieved a hell of a lot! He had led his Yeovil team to win the FA Trophy, become Conference champions and League Two champions, and with Bristol City secured automatic promotion to the Championship.

With the 2007/08 season about to kick off, I was interviewed for a press article about why I'd left Wolves to go to Bristol City, as I knew it had shocked a few Wolves fans. In true journalistic style, my comments were taken out of context, which then pissed off many of the Wolves faithful. I'm still really fucked off about this, and I'm always surprised at how much the press can manipulate a story. I was asked why I'd chosen to leave Wolves to go to Bristol City as on paper, yes, it seemed like a questionable move at the time. Wolves were more established in the Championship and had only been relegated from the Premier League a few seasons earlier. However, apart from being irate with the Wolves chief executive, I truly felt – knowing what I did about GJ and his teams (as well as the fact that Bristol City are backed by billionaire Steve Lansdown) – that Bristol would finish higher than Wolves in the table that season. Only time would tell as to whether my decision to leave Wolves would be justified or not.

I made my debut for Bristol City against QPR at home drawing 2-2 on 11th August 2007. After five games we were sitting at the top of the table and I knew at this point the team were more than capable of being promoted to the Premier League. Although I know most of the pundits and bookmakers would never have agreed this was possible, GJ's magic was definitely rubbing off again.

I scored my first goal for Bristol against Coventry City away, winning 3-0. Several games later I went back to Molineux for the first time since leaving Wolves. I was expecting a frosty reception from the fans, thanks to that press article, but what I actually got was more like an avalanche of abuse for the full 90 minutes. Perhaps if I'd told the true story earlier, they might have directed their abuse towards a certain someone in the home stand. Who knows? The game finished 1-1.

Halfway through the season, we were more than

holding our own. In fact, we were joint top of the table with West Bromwich Albion and Watford.

**

Even though I don't drink, some of the lads invited me out and, as footballers do, we ended up in a strip club. The next thing I knew I was dating a stripper called Sarah. This definitely wasn't one of my finest decisions in life. We had a turbulent relationship and were on and off all the time. I ended up renting her an apartment across from mine. I couldn't handle being woken up in the middle of the night when I had a game the next day.

**

In the January transfer window, we signed Coventry City's Dele Adebola and Australian international Nick Carle. As always I tried to make the new lads feel welcome, particularly Nick and his girlfriend. They didn't have a car due to foreign licensing issues, so I drove them around for a while to help them out.

From 2nd March 2008 in our remaining 11 matches, we won only two, losing our automatic spot we'd held onto throughout the season. We eventually finished 4th securing a play-off spot. I couldn't help but feel the team had fucked up an enormous opportunity to reach the top flight.

In football the biggest jump in standard is from the

Championship to the Premier League, not only financially but also on the pitch. When a club is on the brink of securing promotion to the Premier League, the tension and expectation from everyone rises. It's so important to stick to the ethos and style of play that got you there in the first place. Everybody just wants to get over the line in any way possible. The board members become more anxious due to the financial implications, most managers become irritable and fans start considering what might be. This all filters down to the players and it takes special characters on the pitch to be able to handle that type of pressure as the season comes to a close.

Wolves finished 7th, which I felt justified my previous decision to leave.

Finishing 4th, after just having been promoted from League One, was still a good achievement for Bristol City. This was the second season I had reached the play-off semi-finals and I was deeply disappointed.

GJ called an emergency meeting to make sure the players refocussed on the semi-final against Crystal Palace. The first leg was to be played at Selhurst Park.

In the two games against Palace earlier in the season, they had beaten us 2-0 at Selhurst Park and we had drawn 1-1 at Ashton Gate. Crystal Palace's form going into the match was the complete opposite of ours; they were on a high after losing one in 12 games going into the play-offs. But as we all know, the form guide going into these types of games doesn't mean a thing because the pressure is completely different.

The first half was a tense affair with both teams creating good chances. Shortly into the second half, Louis Carey converted a wonderful set play that GJ had had in his armoury for many years, nicknamed the Weasel. We were trying to hold onto the lead to take back to Ashton Gate, which would have been great, when in 87th minute Palace were awarded a penalty. Ben Watson stepped up and scored, bringing them level, which was a kick in the teeth. With only a few minutes left, the ball was headed down to David Noble, who dropped his shoulder before smashing a 30-yard shot straight into the top corner. The Bristol City fans went crazy. We pinched a 2-1 win, which now gave us the psychological edge going back to the second leg at Ashton Gate.

We had a week to recuperate before facing them again. The result was great; we'd bagged two fantastic goals, but the performance was average. I knew we had more in the tank. The question was, could we bring it out in the second leg and get to Wembley?

Ashton Gate was sold out. The place was rocking. There are certain football grounds around the country that have a huge attendance but very little atmosphere. Ashton Gate's attendance of around 17,000 fans sounds more like 50,000. The ultras behind the goal with their giant banners and red flares enhanced the atmosphere. Whenever we won a game they would celebrate in the pub near the ground, and when any player drove past they'd cheer. If we lost, we took a different route home.

Before the second leg against Crystal Palace you

could sense the nervous energy in the dressing room. I remember pulling aside a few of the players before the game and telling them, "No matter what happens, we have to win."

The game kicked off and we started off strong. 24 minutes in, our goalkeeper Adriano Basso came out to punch but didn't make proper contact, allowing Ben Watson to loop a header back over him into an empty net. It was now 2-2 on aggregate.

The match was more open than in the first leg. In the second half Palace were awarded a penalty. Ben Watson stepped up again but this time missed as the ball came rattling back off the post. It was a key turning point in the match; after this both teams struck the woodwork. With the score still level on aggregate, the game went into extra time. The whole of Bristol were on the edge of their seats.

The ball dropped to an unmarked Lee Trundle who bent it into the top left corner, taking the score to 3-2 on aggregate, igniting the Bristol City fans. In the next 15 minutes somebody's season was about to end.

We had the lead but the game was like a basketball match – end to end and far too open. It was all or nothing. The emotion and pressure were taking their toll on both teams going into the final minutes. We were awarded a free kick about 30 yards from the Palace goal. By now we were obviously trying to waste as much time as possible, but there were still ten minutes to go. I didn't feel comfortable with just doing the usual 'kick the ball into the corner' to let the clock tick down. I remember saying to one of the lads, "Just roll it to me. I'm going to have a shot."

The last thing I wanted was for the ball to ricochet off the wall or for the keeper to catch it and set Palace on the attack. I took a longer run-up than usual and tried to focus on putting as much momentum and power behind the ball as I could. As soon I hit it, I knew it had half a chance. The ball flew into the bottom corner, flying past the Palace goalkeeper Julián Speroni.

It was one of those moments I had re-enacted hundreds of times as a kid on the estate. In those last few minutes of a big game, taking a huge run-up, smashing the ball as hard as you can to score, taking your team to Wembley... For me that moment had just happened.

Until the day I die, I will never forget the noise that erupted from Ashton Gate when the ball hit the back of the net. We won 4-2 on aggregate. The final whistle blew and our ecstatic fans invaded the pitch in celebration.

In the other play-off semi-final, Hull City beat Watford 6-1 over two legs, meaning the date was set for a Wembley showdown on 24th May 2008. Bristol City vs Hull City.

***

The day after the match at Ashton Gate, I was in and out of ice baths which gave me time to reflect on the game. I found myself thinking back to the previous season and my time with Wolves when Mick McCarthy had taken me off in the semi-final against West Bromwich Albion. I'd been furious and during my argument with Mick I'd told him that when the bigger games came around, more often than not, I tended to score. I really hoped he'd watched the Bristol City match on TV and witnessed my late goal.

***

Eight days later, we travelled to our hotel in London for the pre-match build-up. Traditionally, both teams are given the opportunity to visit and walk around the national stadium. Even though the venue was empty, I still felt an adrenaline rush as I took my first steps across the grass. I couldn't believe how huge it was. Pitches vary in size and Wembley is definitely one of the biggest. As I was the one who would be taking corners and free kicks, I found it essential to check out the dimensions of the pitch and the surroundings. I honestly couldn't wait to play!

Hull had secured the England team's choice of hotel, The Grove in Hertfordshire, but we drew the short straw with ours. For such a big match I was surprised the club had chosen what was in my opinion a shitty hotel. It immediately put the players in a bad mood, especially as the food was crap too. Players are trained not to blame anything or anyone other than themselves for poor performances on the pitch, but this is bollocks. Preparation is key to all sporting success.

Tickets for the game had completely sold out. I'd bought 64 tickets for friends and family north and south of the border. Both Bristol and Hull could have filled

Wembley to the brim on their own. The excitement in the lead-up to the game was incredible. This was the biggest game in both clubs' history. Some people aren't aware that the Championship play-off final offers the biggest prize fund in world football, in a single game. If we won that match Bristol City would bag approximately £72 million (although I believe it has now risen to £170 million). I knew the chairman Steve Lansdown was already extremely wealthy but I imagined he would happily have swapped the prize money for a guaranteed spot in the Premier League. Bristol City hadn't been in the top flight in 28 years, and Hull, for all their efforts, had never reached that level.

I never had trouble sleeping before big games but the night before the play-off final I just couldn't get comfortable. It probably had something to do with the foldaway single bed I'd got stuck with, after flipping a coin with my roomy Marvin Elliott. On the morning of the match, Hayden called to wish me luck and couldn't help reminding me that if I lost today I would miss out on around £1.2 million based on my contract terms. We both laughed about it but I knew the financial implications were true. Hayden was in a win-win position as he had a player in each team – me for Bristol City and Caleb Folan for Hull City. He knew that by 5pm another one of his players would be in the Premier League.

As the coach approached Wembley Stadium, all that could be seen was a mass of red and orange. When the lads went out for the warm-up, I stayed behind. Players tend to go out too early and end up wasting a lot of nervous energy on an overly vigorous warm-up due to the occasion. I like to conserve as much energy as I can for the game. Walking out of the tunnel, the heat hit me instantly. The temperature pitchside was in the mid-30s. There's something very special about walking out into Wembley in front of almost 90,000 people. I savoured the moment.

The game kicked off and for the first 20 minutes I tried to get on the ball as much as I could, but every time I touched it Hull City had two players on me. I'd had this before many times in my career and I knew the best thing to do was to move behind the front two strikers. This is a little trick wingers do if they feel the opposition full back and winger are working together to close them down or nullify the supply line to them.

Our right back Bradley Orr had a nasty collision with Nick Barmby, fracturing his cheekbone, but he continued to play on with concussion. This was to come back and haunt us minutes later when Fraizer Campbell broke away down the left. We didn't seem to be in any trouble as we had five defenders against Hull's three attackers, but Brad, being dazed, had left Dean Windass totally free on the edge of the box. Campbell chipped the ball to his teammate and in the 38th minute, Windass smashed an unbelievable right-footed volley into the top corner putting Hull into a 1-0 lead.

During the half-time talk, GJ shouted at the team to step it up. We hadn't really got out of the blocks and I think he realised the stress of the occasion was affecting some of the players.

In the second half we put a lot of pressure on Hull and by now had made 21 attempts at their goal with 13 on target, but we still hadn't scored. Darren Byfield was just inches away from converting a low cross from Ivan Sproule. The game was becoming desperate. I remember purposely crossing three or four balls on top of the goalkeeper Boaz Myhill, hoping Dele Adebola would simply bundle them into the net. We attacked and attacked but to no avail. Seconds later the referee blew the final whistle and most of our players fell to the ground. The opportunity had come and gone so quickly that even when I heard the whistle I still didn't believe we'd lost the match. I felt crushed and defeated. It was one of the most agonising moments in my career. I dropped to my knees and sat on the pitch utterly devastated.

I strongly believed then, and I still do now, that we didn't miss out on the Premier League by losing against Hull City in the play-off final. We lost out on the top flight back in January when we changed our ethos and style of play. GJ's managing style had always been to pass the ball on the floor and attack at speed. In the past he'd always signed players who could handle the ball in tight areas. The free-flowing football I was accustomed to playing under him had changed drastically. He didn't reinforce the style of play that had got us there in the first place. This is what high levels of pressure can do to managers.

23
I'm No Politician

After the match, I went upstairs to meet Hayden who was sitting with James Brown, the co-founder of Loaded magazine. As we started to discuss the match, Caleb Folan came over. We all congratulated him on Hull City's win. I thought it was extremely respectful of him to say he didn't want to celebrate in front of me, but I told him to fuck off as he'd earned it.

It was a magnificent moment for Dean Windass who, at 40 years of age, born and bred in Hull, scored the winning goal at Wembley taking his team into the Premier League for the first time.

Throughout the course of the campaign, I was surprised and disappointed I hadn't been called up again for the national team. I'd finished a long, hard season with 49 games and seven goals. It was good but I should have scored more. Either way, GJ didn't fuck around this time and rewarded me with a new three-year contract. We also discussed the possibility of bringing in my old pal Gavin Williams, as the club had just sold Nick Carle to Crystal Palace. This was in my opinion probably Bristol City's best ever bit of business. Selling one of our attacking players who'd never scored a goal for £1 million and signing Gavin for a reported £100,000, who was twice the player Nick would ever be.

After some summer sun, I returned a few days early to meet Gav just as we were about to sign him from Ipswich Town. It was brilliant news and I have no doubt that if he'd played the previous season we would have been automatically promoted. We had a good chance this season to right our wrongs. We also signed Nicky Maynard from Crewe Alexandra for £2.5 million, proving that the chairman Steve Lansdown was still keen to seek promotion. His passion for his club and city always reminded me of how John Ryan was; he also used to come down to see us before every home game and say a few words to boost confidence in the dressing room.

Before a ball is even kicked in the Championship there is a 25% chance that you will either be relegated or promoted, so going into my second season with Bristol City I knew it would be harder. The play-off final had definitely knocked the stuffing out of a few of the lads, but the beautiful thing about football is you always get another chance to prove yourself. Players who had sneaked under the radar in the previous season now had to step up again. After reaching the semi-finals with Wolves, then the final with Bristol City, I was hoping it would be third time lucky and we would achieve automatic promotion.

Four games into the 2008/09 season, it was clear that the play-off final defeat hadn't affected the team excessively, as we were sitting joint 2nd in the table with Wolves. We had just beaten Coventry City 3-0 away and I'd got on the score sheet.

A couple of weeks later we played Doncaster Rovers at home. I'd exchanged a bit of banter with my old friend John Ryan, chairman of Doncaster, who jokingly asked me not to score against them that day. I went on to score two goals, winning 4-1. It's always a good feeling scoring against an old team.

Ten games in, we dropped down to 6th place. The team lacked the synergy we'd had in the first half of the previous season, but I knew once Gav bedded in, it would be better. There were some murmurs in the dressing room because GJ was turning up the heat on a few of the new signings in training. Nicky Maynard had only scored two goals in his first 17 games since his move from Crewe and his first big-money contract. Aware of GJ's style of bombarding players with verbal attacks to test their character, I knew Nicky wasn't the kind of person to respond to this type of management. The more GJ pushed him, the more Nicky's confidence dipped.

In a match against Sheffield Wednesday away, Nicky missed a one-vs-one with the goalkeeper in the last minute. We drew 0-0. In the dressing room after the match, GJ tore into Nicky blaming the result solely on his miss. I remember looking across at the young 21 year-old who was almost in tears, thinking that the poor fucker was already distraught enough from missing the chance. We'd all had loads of chances to polish Sheffield off and all of our performances had been bang average. So to single the youngster out was wrong. I didn't like it and I said so at the time in front of everybody.

I had a long chat with Nicky on the coach during the journey back to Bristol. I told him GJ had done the exact same thing to me while I was at Yeovil. I think I was even the same age. I said it wasn't personal and the best way to cope with it was to use the old trick I'd used. As soon as GJ started to shout, just give him the thumbs up in agreement to shut him up. It was funny watching GJ's face every time Nicky followed my advice. It worked, though, and he went on to score five goals in the next five matches.

As I became a more seasoned professional I ensured I took the time to speak to younger players to try to give them solid advice about the industry and its pitfalls.

At the halfway point of the season, we were sitting in the bottom half of the table in 14th place. GJ wasn't selecting certain players, which I found strange. We'd had a decent start to the season but the more games we played the further down the table we slipped. To make matters worse, Wolves were flying high at the top of the Championship. Any player who says they don't give a fuck about how their old team is doing is a liar. I definitely wanted to be at the top of the table. I was hoping the Christmas period might bring a change in fortune.

A few days after Christmas we played Crystal Palace at home. Nicky scored just two minutes in, after Stern John found him on the edge of the box. We outplayed Palace in the first half. The game was becoming a little nasty with a few late tackles flying in. Midway through the second half I had a shot from the edge of the box, which went just wide of the post. As I turned around a Palace player elbowed me on the chin. It was my ex-teammate Nick Carle. I stuck my head into his face. He started mouthing off. I wasn't too bothered, as sometimes that kind of behaviour is just down to the intensity of the game, but when he started being disrespectful about my family it riled me. Only five months earlier I'd driven him and his girlfriend around Bristol to help them out while they didn't have a car. I've learnt over the years that when players try to wind me up on the pitch, more often than not they end up just winding themselves up. Two minutes later I got the ball and nutmegged him to piss him off.

The game finished 1-0. We'd beaten them again.

Coincidently, as I was coming into the tunnel so was Nick Carle. I couldn't help but look at the little cunt and remember what he'd said to me on the pitch. There were a few scuffles on the way into the dressing room. It was later alleged I'd thrown a bottle in the direction of Nick's face.

Once the handbags had settled down, my teammate Cole Skuse jokingly tried to provoke me, saying that Nick would have had me. I bet him £20 he was wrong.

Coincidently again, I bumped into Nick Carle in the players' car park as he went to get on the Crystal Palace coach. It didn't take long before an altercation broke out. The funny thing was that while Nick and I were trading blows, his teammates were already on the coach. Within seconds, half the Palace football team came to help him. Obviously I took a pounding and spent that night having my nose glued back together in A&E.

The next morning I went into training and collected

my £20 from Cole Skuse. I went on to play Nick Carle again later in my career but he didn't ever say another word to me, the silly little cunt.

I found out later, from a Crystal Palace player who was in the dressing room that day, that Neil Warnock may have suggested to Nick that he should try to wind me up.

We played Wolves at Molineux, losing 2-0, and as usual the Wolves fans sang nice songs about me! After the game the press asked me what the difference was between Wolves and Bristol City this season. Wolves were sat at the top of the Championship and we were in a measly 14th position. I was very frank in my opinion. I said the players we'd signed in the last two transfer windows (excluding Gav) were nowhere near as good as the players Wolves had signed in the same period. This didn't go down too well with the board at Bristol City or with GJ, who put a media ban on me until further notice. I felt it was just an honest appraisal. The following match we played Plymouth away in a West Country derby and GJ dropped me to the bench.

I get really pissed off when football clubs have asked me to speak to the press to give my opinion but then because I've been honest, I find myself on the bench. I'm a footballer not a politician.

On the odd occasion that I found myself on the bench, I always did what John Moore taught me many years ago when I was trying to break through into the first team at Luton. The manager has seven subs but can only use three. If a game is going to plan, it's unlikely a manager will make a substitution unless it's a tactical decision. If it isn't going to plan or a player gets injured, he will look at the options he has available to him. Motionless subs will not be at the forefront of the gaffer's mind, so I'd make sure I was constantly in sight. I'd run up and down the touchline in front of him blocking his view of the game. Every ten minutes I'd remind him I was ready to go on. Most players I knew would just sit on the bench feeling sorry for themselves and only warm up because they were told to.

In the first half of the match against Plymouth, even though the rain was hammering down I still left the dugout to do my 'get off the bench' routine. It worked. GJ put me on after 41 minutes for Marvin Elliott. Fifteen minutes into the second half I blocked a clearance from a Plymouth defender and the ball broke kindly for me, enabling me to drill it into the bottom corner. I ran behind the goal to celebrate with the Bristol City fans. We went on to win 2-0.

Gav and I both scored the following week against Barnsley at home, winning 2-0 again. The win had put us up to 11th place and we were only seven points away from a play-off spot with a game in hand. We also went on to win our next three matches, which was no surprise as Gav had started to settle in. We'd now moved up to 7th in the table and were only one point away from a play-off spot.

***

At training, our captain Louis Carey pulled me aside to have a chat. I could tell by his face it wasn't football related. It was about Sarah. He told me she'd been playing up and he felt compelled to let me know. I'd always valued his friendship and loyalty so trusted what he was telling me.

Sarah and I had been dating on and off for the last year or so. Her lifestyle and job were not for me. I'd tried on many occasions to understand her choices and help her to change her path, but clearly without any joy. That week I called it a day.

***

With eight games to go we were joint 6th with Swansea City. If we could win half of our remaining matches I thought we might finish in the play-offs again. The problem was, GJ was chopping and changing the team constantly. I didn't understand why as we were now at the business end of the season and teams who get promoted tend to have a settled line-up.

During a crossing and finishing session at training, GJ had a bee in his bonnet about something. Maybe the stress was taking its toll but whatever it was, it caused him to take it out on the team.

The ball was whipped in for Lee Trundle, who headed it but missed the target. GJ went mental and blamed the miss on the beanie hat Trunds was wearing. He wore a hat most days, especially on colder mornings. A short while later a cross came in from the other side of the pitch and as Trunds went to head it, his hat slipped over his eyes. Unable to see, the ball hit the side of his head and he missed the goal again. GJ was furious and told Trunds to fuck off and train on his own, pointing him towards the adjacent pitch.

Two minutes later I misplaced a pass and found myself on the other pitch with Trunds. Slowly but surely GJ started to run out of players to moan at as most of us were now standing on the next pitch. The senior lads, including myself, were beginning to question what was going on in his head. Private discussions were happening all over the place. I received phone calls from the board at Bristol City asking if these training incidents were true.

The captain felt it was appropriate to approach GJ's son Lee, to see if he could shed some light on the situation, but unfortunately he couldn't.

GJ's outbursts aside, the thing that was still bothering me the most was the type of football we were playing. It wasn't the style he used to preach about previously. Out of our last eight matches we hadn't won a single game! The pattern was almost identical to the previous season. In the final five to ten matches in any season, you truly discover who your real winners are – the players with the most ambition, the hungriest, the ones who will sacrifice the most to succeed, and those who enjoy being in the pressure pot. We had to beat Swansea City away to keep any hopes of a play-off spot alive. But we lost the game 1-0, effectively ending our season. I overheard two of my own teammates, Bradley Orr and Jamie McAllister, talking about their summer holiday destinations before they'd even left the pitch. I was fuming. We hadn't won the match so I certainly didn't have the mindset to talk about where the fuck I was going to go on holiday!

I felt a lot of players in the dressing room had bottled it again. I was angry all summer. We finished 10th. I'd played 48 games, and frequently been placed in centre midfield so I only scored six goals. As far as I was concerned it was a shit season. To rub more salt into the wound, Wolves were deservedly crowned Champions and promoted to the Premier League.

The season ended and I still had two years left on my Bristol City contract but I wanted to move on. I didn't feel the team were moving in the right direction. GJ knew how I felt. He thought it would be better if I did my own training and concentrated on going to a new club. A few days later Bristol City accepted a fee in the region of £500,000 from Sheffield United. GJ gave me permission to speak to the manager Kevin Blackwell. I arranged to drive up to Sheffield later in the week to meet him.

I can honestly say it was the strangest meeting I've ever had with a football manager. We sat down in his office at Bramall Lane and after five minutes he started asking some very odd questions, like what would happen if he didn't play me? I told him he wouldn't have a reason not to play me, but if that were the case I'd work hard to get back in the team. I sat there wondering why I'd bothered going to see him if he was already thinking about dropping me from the team!

I'd played for eight football clubs and talked to numerous managers over the years. To be asked what would happen if I wasn't selected before I'd even fucking signed, bamboozled me! I felt the meeting had a very negative tone to it. I'd just driven for four and half hours up the motorway to see this weirdo. I thought we'd be discussing positive football topics about the coming season, or he'd at least be trying to entice me to the club by telling me how great a city Sheffield is.

On the way back down the M5, I called Hayden to express my concern. He told me Kevin Blackwell had wanted to meet me before we put pen to paper. I thought that was fair enough. He seemed strange but Sheffield United was a club I'd always wanted to sign for.

I spent the first few weeks of pre-season training on my own with Sean Veira at his MMA gym in Clifton. He was a three times World Kickboxing Champion. I would get up in the morning and run to his gym where we would spend two hours on strength and conditioning before finishing the morning session sparring. In the afternoon we would concentrate on football-specific exercises, based on speed and agility. It was brutal but soon I was in the best shape I'd ever been in.

A week or so later I spoke with Kevin Blackwell on the phone. We discussed arranging personal terms and he assured me it would be done the following week. Hayden seemed confident so I continued my training with Sean.

I had heard that Sheffield United were about to leave to go on their pre-season trip to Malta. It had now been two weeks since I'd travelled to Sheffield. Usually, whenever I'd been given permission to speak to another club, Hayden and I had thrashed out personal terms within 48 hours and signed a contract. I knew something wasn't right. I called Kevin Blackwell who was at the airport. I asked him what was delaying the deal. He said something about the board and money, but not to worry as it would be sorted out once he was back.

After hanging up the telephone, I didn't feel confident so I rang my old coach from Luton, John Moore, for advice. I explained the situation and he told me in no uncertain terms to pull out of the deal. John had been a player, a coach and a manager, so he'd seen it all in his time. He told me it was obvious that Kevin Blackwell had identified a few players for the same position and was keeping us all on hold until he chose one. It made complete sense. I thanked John and called Hayden to tell him I was pulling out of the deal. Hayden agreed that something wasn't right and advised me to ring GJ. He assured me that other Championship clubs would make an offer now the Sheffield United deal was on its arse, and to sit tight.

I called GJ to let him know my plans and he agreed it should have been finalised by now. Sean was keeping me in great shape but I still needed to maintain my match fitness. GJ decided it would be best for both parties if I were put back in the squad for Bristol City's pre-season friendly against Martin Jol's AFC Ajax.

What I witnessed in the first half was a true spectacle of passing excellence and I'm glad GJ only brought me on in the second half! I think the possession stats must have been at least 80% in favour of Ajax. They were cutting us open at will. Luis Suárez put Ajax ahead at 27 minutes with a lovely finish. I think it was 3-0 when GJ brought me on, just after one of their players had scored a 45-yard chip over the goalkeeper. I knew by the way the game was going I wouldn't see much of the ball, but I used it as a fitness exercise. Still to this day, I've never seen a team annihilate another professional team like Ajax did that evening. GJ had just made some new signings and watching the team's performance didn't fill me with much confidence about staying at Bristol.

24
Is the Sky Blue?

The season would start in ten days. Never one to doubt Hayden, I sat tight and as usual he was right. Coventry City put a bid in for approximately £325,000 including add-ons. Bristol City accepted their offer and GJ pulled me aside after training to inform me. The following day I drove to Coventry to meet Hayden. He knew the manager Chris Coleman through the late legend, Gary Speed. If they wanted my signature they would have to better my current contract with Bristol City as I still had around £1 million tied up in it.

Coventry was relegated from the Premier League in 2001. They'd been in the Championship ever since so in my eyes they were a stable Championship club. Hayden spoke very highly of Chris Coleman and knowing us both, thought we would get along.

An hour or so later we drove across to the Ricoh Arena to meet Chris and the then chairman Ray Ranson. Straightaway the gaffer and I clicked so we left Hayden and the chairman to thrash out the money talks, while we went to discuss football. Chris showed me around the stadium and its notable facilities. The place boasted a hotel, its own casino, indoor arena and restaurants. It was extremely impressive.

Hayden and the chairman finally came to an agreement based on a two-year contract. I was now Coventry City's new left winger. The gaffer gave me the next day off and I was to report back on Thursday for a fitness test. Our season kicked off that coming Sunday, 9th August 2009 with a televised match against Ipswich Town at home.

Obviously I passed the fitness test and was straight into the starting line-up for Sunday's match. I hadn't had much time to get to know my new teammates but it made no difference as we won 2-1.

***

From 2003 until 2009 I'd signed nine football contracts, totalling a time-span of around 23 years. I don't believe any other player in the UK has signed more contracts than me, exceeding this many years in this space of time. Hayden and I formed a formidable partnership. The advice I would always give to up-and-coming young footballers is to make sure you find an agent who doesn't blow smoke up your arse – one who will be your biggest critic, but most importantly one who understands the game on and off the field. An agent needs to have a vast array of contacts, including players, coaches, managers, chief scouts, chief executives, chairmen and other agents throughout the footballing world. The industry is ridiculously close-knit. Hayden had all of these.

***

Ten games into the 2009/10 season we couldn't find much consistency and we were 13th in the league. The club was paying a fortune to players who in my opinion were just deadwood. In the dressing room, they were more interested in who had the best car, or the best-looking girl on their arm, or who was getting paid the most. If they'd channelled that level of competitiveness into what was happening on the pitch, then we might have got somewhere. The gaffer needed to have a clear-out. I think he already knew this, but it was going to take time to bring the team up to scratch.

I missed a match against Leicester City at home. My knee had swollen up like a balloon after getting kicked in the previous game against Watford. I spent the week on the physio bed. The gaffer came in to let me know I'd been called up for Scotland in a match against Japan. I wasn't fit and hadn't been playing for my own club so although I was itching to play, I knew full well I wouldn't be up to it. The match was in Japan. I wasn't going to travel all that way to hobble around and make a twat of myself, so the gaffer made the necessary calls for me.

Over the next ten league games we'd slipped further down the table to 20th. We had numerous players in the dressing room with a lot of attitude who would use their teammates as scapegoats. Players know the type: individuals who deflect their own mistakes onto other people. It felt like it was every man for himself rather than being a team effort.

Off the pitch I'd reached a ten-year milestone of being teetotal. It must have been a good omen as we won our next three matches, but our following games were a grind and we struggled to show any real form. Over the next 16 matches I don't know how the fuck we did it, but we'd managed to climb painstakingly back up to 8th position. Our upcoming game was at home against Cardiff City who were in 6th position, two points above us. If we could beat them we would sneak into a play-off spot with nine games to go.

During the match I went to kick the ball up the line to Jon Stead and I felt a sharp shooting pain in the left side of my stomach. I didn't think much of it until five minutes later when I went to take a corner. As soon as I crossed the ball into the box I felt an even sharper pain. I knew instantly I'd ripped a muscle. I tried to play on for another few minutes but every time I made a sudden movement I could feel it rip even more. The pain was excruciating. After 46 minutes I told the physio I had to come off. It was 1-1 at the time and I knew how important the game was to turn our season around. Watching the second half but being unable to contribute was horrible. As the game came to a close, Cardiff were awarded a penalty and Peter Whittingham stepped up and scored. We lost 2-1.

I missed the next five games due to my torn stomach muscle. I was unbearable company. I hated not playing. Some players were used to getting injured but I'd been extremely lucky. Over the last decade I'd only missed around a dozen games due to injury or suspension. It might have been due to the fact that I spent most Sunday mornings in an ice bath freezing my bollocks off, but I have no doubt that not drinking alcohol was also a huge contributing factor.

After the Cardiff City game we didn't win another game that season and plummeted down the table to finish 19th.

I signed for Coventry expecting to be scoring goals and creating chances for others, as I'd done for many years. Instead over the course of the season I'd played in every position except right back and in goal. I didn't mind filling in gaps for the gaffer, I knew he needed help and time to develop the squad, but looking back it was extremely detrimental to both me and the team. I scored one goal in 43 games – my worst goal contribution for many years. The season was a rollercoaster. This was also the first time in my career I'd finished in the bottom half of any league after a full season at a club.

Two days after our last game the gaffer was sacked. I personally thought it was the wrong decision by the board. He'd spent the last two seasons getting rid of most of the deadwood and was never really given any decent money to bring in top players.

It had been a very disappointing season, and I left to go on holiday to Spain for the summer. It was there I met my new girlfriend, model Emma Frain, a northern girl who despite her looks was very down to earth.

At the start of the 2010/11 campaign, Coventry City

had appointed Aidy Boothroyd as their new manager. Returning to Coventry for the pre-season, he called a meeting with the entire squad. I think a few of the lads were sceptical as he was renowned for playing the long ball game. Aidy's first job was to take us to Obertraun in Austria to a training camp coordinated by David Moyes' brother, Kenny.

A day or so into training, I asked Aidy if I could be the captain for the new season ahead and I also discussed my contract situation. I had one year left on my current deal and this was uncharted territory for me. Aidy told me there were already a couple of names in the hat, including mine, but he would make a decision on the new captain when we returned to the UK. This seemed fair because as yet he hadn't had any time to look at the squad properly.

While in Austria, we played our first pre-season friendly against VF Gaflenz. Aidy named me captain before the match, which was a good sign. It wasn't the first time I'd had the armband at a club, but this time I wanted it permanently. We won the match 2-0.

After the team arrived back in the UK, I decided to pop my head into Aidy's office before training to ask about the captaincy and my new contract. He told me he was choosing somebody else as captain and he wouldn't be offering me a new contract. Then, to my absolute amazement, he also said I wouldn't be playing for him all season, without giving any explanation.

I was in total disbelief. The captain's armband and the new contract I could get my head around, as those choices are of course his prerogative, but ask any player who has ever played with me since leaving Luton Town and I hope they'd all agree that I'm always one of the fittest, most professional and one of the hungriest footballers they have played alongside. For this man to tell me after one bullshit pre-season game that I wouldn't play all season was a fucking disgrace! I'd never worked with Aidy Boothroyd before, so it wasn't as if we'd formerly clashed. Something was definitely not right and I made it my mission to get to the bottom of it.

On the training ground I made sure I continued to train with my usual high intensity and focus. I wasn't going to let this little manager bring my standards down, no matter what his problem was.

The season kicked off and I wasn't even in the fucking squad. This was the first time since being a kid that I was fit yet not selected. I wouldn't have minded if I was at Real Madrid but I wasn't; I was at Coventry City and one of the most experienced, highest-paid players in the dressing room at a struggling club. More importantly I had proved myself in terms of scoring, setting up goals and causing the opposition problems in the Championship. I was fully fit and raring to go.

I asked Hayden to speak to him and attempt to discover what the problem really was. When Hayden called me back he said Aidy was being vague and not giving any actual answers.

The following game was a Carling Cup match at home where Aidy put me back into the starting line-up alongside all the kids. Needless to say we lost. He was to leave me out of the squad again for the next three consecutive league matches.

After a home match I saw my old Doncaster Rovers manager, Dave Penney, walking through the dressing room and into Aidy's office. My fellow teammate Sammy Clingan, who was aware of my history with Dave, looked at me and laughed at the expression on my face. In his Northern Irish accent, Sammy told me I was fucked, and that was probably the reason I wasn't playing.

I didn't know Dave and Aidy were buddies. If that was the case, I knew Aidy wasn't going to be doing me any favours.

We played Leicester City at home and Aidy named me as a substitute. After 35 minutes Gary McSheffrey incurred an injury. I was the only winger on the bench, so Aidy had no choice but to begrudgingly put me on. After four minutes of being on the pitch, I set up the opening goal, crossing for Clive Platt who bulleted home a header. The match finished 1-1. Aidy didn't say a single word to me after the game.

I knew I had applied the pressure. So guess what Aidy rewarded me with? Not playing me again for the next 11 matches.

The team were starting to moan about Aidy's tactics and style of play. We spent most of the week in training, practising goal kicks and set plays. Aidy would ask the goalkeeper Kieren Westwood to boot the ball up the pitch while the rest of us stood around like robots being told where to stand and what to do. Players don't mind doing one session a week on set plays, as we know the importance of them. But to do this almost every day is soul-destroying. Day by day I could see the lads becoming more and more pissed off. They were complaining more than I was, and they were playing!

During one of Aidy's riveting training sessions, Kieren kicked the ball long into the channel. Aidy stopped everyone immediately to instruct the midfielders to turn and run if the ball went over their head. No shit, Sherlock. I looked at Lee Carsley and tried not to laugh. I was being asked every day why Aidy wasn't playing me, particularly by the strikers. I honestly couldn't give them a straight answer, as I genuinely didn't know myself. All I could assume was that Dave Penney's influence had rubbed off.

Despite how angry I was, I made a huge statement by not letting this bullshit bring my mood down. I was always the first man on the training pitch and the last to leave. In fact I spent most afternoons practising free kicks outside Aidy's office window. With so many hopeful young footballers in the dressing room, it was important to me that I retained my professionalism by setting a good example. I knew this wouldn't go unnoticed.

In a game away against Ipswich Town, I was on the bench when Coventry was awarded a corner. Aidy sprung from the dugout screaming at the players to lock them in and something about a three-quarter press? Roy Keane turned to Aidy with a look on his face that mirrored my own thoughts, "What the fuck is this guy on about?"

It made me chuckle. I have no idea what coaching manual Aidy was reading – and by the look on Roy Keane's face, nor did he.

Hayden thought he knew the reason why Aidy wasn't playing me. He said it might be due to a clause in the transfer contract between Bristol City and Coventry. Coventry would be legally bound to pay Bristol City money every time I hit a certain number of starting league appearances. If this was the case and the club were strapped for cash, I still didn't understand why Aidy wouldn't just explain the situation to me. After all, it's not the manager's money and we could have tried to come up with another idea to ensure I could still help the team.

Speaking to Aidy was a waste of time. I tried to ring the chairman Ray Ranson on several occasions, but it would have been easier to find a postman on a Sunday than it was to reach him.

Emma asked me if I ever actually played football, or did Coventry just pay me all this money to do nothing? I laughed because someone with zero football knowledge had also realised how ludicrous the scenario was.

One morning before training started I went upstairs to knock on Aidy's door. I wanted some straight answers. I asked him outright if it was because of the clause between the two clubs or the fact that he was Dave Penney's pal.

Aidy stuttered, trying to avoid giving me a direct answer. I felt like punching him on his chin. I told him if he wasn't going to start playing me in league games I would play football elsewhere. He said no problem, but I would never be allowed to go on loan to another Championship club. Funny that! Dave Penney had said exactly the same thing. What a fucking wanker. It summed Aidy up perfectly. I slammed the door as I walked out of his office.

I unloaded my thoughts about Aidy onto Clive Platt in the dressing room. He told me a friend of his would probably be keen to take me to MK Dons on loan. I just wanted to play! I asked Platty to tell his friend to call Aidy straight away. It was highly possible that MK Dons wouldn't have to pay any of my wages as Coventry City was being run so poorly and liked wasting money.

***

I made my debut for MK Dons in a 2-0 win against Brentford away. I spent most of the second half playing up front. It was such a relief to be playing football and to be on the pitch again. I had a big smile on my face.

My old pal Jude Stirling was also playing there, so it was great to see him again. There was never a dull moment in a dressing room when he was around. I went on to play the next seven matches during my short loan spell at MK Dons, which served its purpose of boosting my match fitness. There were discussions between the two clubs about extending the loan period until the end of the season. However, with no disrespect to MK Dons, I didn't want to be applying my trade in League One at that point in my career.

I returned to Coventry City in January 2011. I went to

see Aidy and said that if there was any clause holding me back, I would offer to forfeit my wages so that I could start some league matches. If I were a manager, I would have jumped at the chance and called the board immediately to see if this was even possible. But not Aidy. He felt it was more appropriate to do nothing and leave me out of the squad for a further two months despite Coventry slipping down the table at a tremendous speed.

I remember a conversation we had in late February on the training ground. I told Aidy he needed to do something. Coventry wasn't Watford and he'd be sacked unless the results started to change. I reiterated that I was ready to play and help the team. Throughout the last few weeks I'd been travelling to the away matches on my own just to watch. I wanted to stay on top of what was happening on the pitch and give some of the younger lads feedback on a Monday morning. Believe me, not many footballers would do this.

My boot boy that season was the young Callum Wilson. He must have been the happiest boot boy in the world with no boots to clean at the weekend. Callum trained with the first team a lot. He was a very talented young player and I used to wonder why he'd only ever been involved twice with the first team. He was already showing up some of our senior defenders on the training ground.

By the middle of March, Aidy had won only one of his last 16 league matches and we'd slipped to 19th place, just seven points clear of the relegation zone. Aidy was sacked after a mere 10 months, on 14th March 2011.

Ray Ranson appointed chief scout Andy Thorn as temporary manager. The following day the new gaffer immediately put me back in the squad. He also confirmed that a clause did exist in the contract between Bristol and Coventry. Financially the club was struggling. I completely understood their position. Andy assured me I would be in every squad until the end of the season. He would bring me on from the bench as much as he could without making it too obvious to the fans. Finally, some much-appreciated honesty!

Aidy Boothroyd once said, "Professional footballers should be professional." The next time I bump into Aidy, I'm going to ask him if he feels he was professional during his short-lived time as the manager at Coventry City.

Throughout this period I spoke to Hayden regularly to make him fully aware of the dark cloud that was hanging over the football club. If they could not afford to pay what was in Championship terms a small amount of money, enabling me to start, I knew this club was on a rapid decline. I couldn't wait to get out of there. The rosy picture Ray Ranson had painted when he initially signed me was clearly not a true reflection of the real financial situation.

Andy Thorn did an admirable job in his first managerial post, only losing two out of the last ten matches of the season, and steering Coventry City 13 points clear of relegation. He stuck firmly to his word and brought me onto the pitch as much as he could.

As a parting gift, and to thank me for my professionalism throughout, Andy allowed me to finish the season a week early. A couple of days later I drove to St James' Park in Exeter to play with Yeovil Town XI in a match against Exeter City, in memory of my late teammate Adam Stansfield. It was great to see some old Yeovil faces and both clubs paying tribute to such a lovely man.

I didn't realise it at the time but this was to be my last match and the day I hung up my football boots.

***

I was very lucky and extremely blessed to have lived my dream, playing for ten professional football clubs over 15 years, with no relegations or serious injuries. I have played with some brilliant footballers and learnt a great deal about how and how not to manage. My career has been challenging but incredibly rewarding.

Schoolboy

Salvesdon Boys Club
Hutchison Vale Boys Club
Hibernian FC
Musselburgh Union Boys Club

Youth

1996/1997	Luton Town FC
1997/1998	Luton Town FC

Senior

Season	Club	Appearances	Goals
1998/1999	Luton Town FC	27	0
1999/2000	Luton Town FC	20	0
2000/2001	Hereford United FC	30	2
2000/2001	Yeovil Town FC	16	3
2001/2002	Yeovil Town FC	44	9
2002/2003	Yeovil Town FC	50	13
2003/2004	Doncaster Rovers FC	50	10
2004/2005	Doncaster Rovers FC	51	12
2005/2006	Doncaster Rovers FC	41	13
2005/2006	Derby County FC	8	0
2006/2007	Barnsley FC	20	5
2006/2007	Wolverhampton Wanderers FC	32	3
2007/2008	Bristol City FC	49	7
2008/2009	Bristol City FC	48	6
2009/2010	Coventry City FC	43	1
2010/2011	MK Dons FC	8	0
2010/2011	Coventry City FC	7	0
TOTAL*		544	84

*Domestic league/cup appearances and goals

International

2003-2006	Scotland	2	0

Honours

- Championship Play-Off Final Runner-Up: 2007/2008
- Championship Play-Off Semi-Finalist: 2006/2007
- PFA Team of the Year League One: 2005/2006
- Carling Cup Quarter-Finalist: 2005/2006
- League One Player of the Month: Dec 2005
- Five Footballers of the Year, The Times Football Yearbook 2004-05
- Doncaster Rovers Player of the Year: 2003/2004
- PFA Team of the Year Division Three: 2003/2004
- PFA Third Division Player of the Year: 2003/2004
- Football League Division Three Champion: 2003/2004
- Nationwide Conference Player of the Year: 2002/2003
- Nationwide Conference Champion: 2002/2003
- Yeovil Town Player of the Year: 2002/2003
- Nationwide Conference Team of the Year: 2002/2003
- FA Trophy Winner: 2001/2002
- Yeovil Town Players' Player of the Year: 2001/2002
- South East Counties Youth League Cup Winner: 1997/1998
- FA Youth Cup Semi-Finalist: 1996/1997

Part III

Chinese Whispers

25
Change of Direction

Throughout my career I'd spent hours and hours preparing for matches. It was a military-style dedicated routine of hydration, diet, sleep, training, ice baths, no smoking, no drinking and no sex before a match. Everything I did was to make sure I was 100% ready. I've made a lot of sacrifices over the years but because I absolutely loved playing football, most of these sacrifices were easy. The feeling I got in the pit of my stomach when I woke up on a match day, the atmosphere when I walked out onto the pitch, the sound of the crowd when I scored or set up a goal made it all worthwhile. So I cannot express how deflating and depressing it was to be told week after week, for almost an entire season, that I wasn't allowed to play and all I could do was fucking watch. I'd always prided myself on knowing that I'd played the greatest number of matches possible, and to end the season as I did was truly disheartening.

I knew I wouldn't have any problems in securing a new contract somewhere else but I'd seriously started to consider a life outside football and the possibility of completely changing my career path. I decided I'd use my closed season break in Marbella to think about what I wanted to do at this stage of my life.

My Coventry City teammate Clive Platt had

previously introduced me to another former footballer and his Cypriot associate Mr G. While I was in Marbella, Mr G came to see me at my villa about a potential deal involving a London nightclub. I was interested but at the same time unsure as I didn't know anything about running a nightclub. I was, however, open to new suggestions. I wouldn't have entertained the idea of going ahead with that meeting had it not been for the fact that they'd been recommended to me by a fellow footballer whom I trusted.

Mr G was a funny little chap who walked like a penguin. I thought he looked older than he was; he was only in his mid-thirties. He had a lot of charisma and was easy to get along with. We discussed a deal whereby I would buy 50% of the shares in a central London nightclub on Dean Street called Maya. There were four years left on the lease but Mr G assured me this could be extended. They explained that current shareholders would also need to be bought out and Mr G would construct the deal between them for a fee. Obviously I would need to see the premises and I would be throwing myself into a completely new venture, but I was definitely interested.

I'd always fancied the idea of running my own nightclub – ironic, though, seeing as I don't drink! I also felt I could add value to the business due to my extensive list of contacts and the fact that I'd organised successful events in the past. I liked the idea and it filled me with an excitement I'd not experienced for a while. So without much hesitation, I told them my accountant would be in touch with the solicitor to start the due diligence process.

In the meantime, a couple of Championship clubs had shown an interest in signing me. I still wasn't sure if I was ready to leave football. The discussions about running the nightclub were still in their earliest stages and I wanted to think about all my options. It was the first time in 11 years that I'd been a free agent. Yet Hayden felt I was at the peak of my career and could play for another 10 years as I was in very good shape and extremely fit. He thought I was crazy to even contemplate leaving the industry, but he said that ultimately the decision was mine.

I'd been doing the same thing for the last 15 years. I suppose I wanted to see what life was like beyond training and weekly matches. So after considerable thought, I decided I was ready to take a break and keen to rise to a different challenge.

I like to be 'hands on' and involved, so if I went ahead and bought the shares I planned on moving down to London – a prospect that not only excited me but Emma too. Her modelling agency was based a stone's throw from the nightclub in Soho and most of her castings were in London, so moving there would definitely further her career.

Every discussion I'd had with Mr G had been verbal up to this point, and before I signed any documents I still needed to see the venue. But unless I found I didn't like its location, which was unlikely, or unless the numbers didn't add up, I felt confident the deal would go ahead.

We decided to have a pre-celebration at one of Ocean Club's famous champagne spray parties in Marbella. I was

31 years old and about to become the majority shareholder of a central London nightclub! It was an extremely exciting time for me. I needed to shake off the last season too, and this was the perfect opportunity for me to unwind.

You've probably seen those pictures in the papers. The ones they've rehashed time and time again. Of course I was enjoying myself – I was having a fucking great time! No, I wasn't drinking. Yes, I raised my hands in the air while being soaked in champagne. Yes, I was smoking a cigar. And yes, I sprayed a few bottles of champagne just as everyone else did that day. That's the whole point of a spray party. I was just about to buy a nightclub and I was celebrating. But everything else that was printed is bullshit!

When the summer ended I returned to the UK. Mr G was quick to organise a viewing of the nightclub and he arranged for me to stay in the Mayfair Hotel, close to Soho where the club was based.

A few years earlier the club, formerly known as Maya, had been 'the place to be seen' and it had had a large celebrity following, but since then there had been a significant amount of trouble. The clientele had changed considerably. The venue needed refurbishing and a fresh new look to attract the kind of clientele I had in mind. The interiors were dated. I could see it had potential but needed some serious money thrown at it if it were to compete with its London rivals. It was agreed that a new name and concept would give it a new lease of life. I really liked what I saw. It was a big commercial project and nothing like I'd ever taken on before, but I was more excited than daunted by the challenge.

During the due diligence process my accountant raised concerns about several missing documents. When I asked Mr G about them, he assured me they would arrive within a few days. Although my accountant wasn't keen on the deal, some documents did arrive so I was eager to complete.

The deal eventually went through around mid-July 2011. Some funds were transferred to Mr G's recommended London-based law firm and on top of this a substantial amount of money was paid to Mr G for constructing the deal. I was now the majority shareholder with a 50% stake in the business. One of Mr G's associates owned a 42.5% shareholding and another of his associates owned a 7.5% shareholding. It had been agreed with the other shareholders that we would shut the club down the very next day to start stripping it out and we would split the renovation costs between us.

In the same month I set up a concierge business, Huxley of London. Mr G showed me around a couple of serviced offices in Mayfair – potential bases for the new business – and I chose one on Berkeley Square. The concept was to create a concierge service aimed at giving my contacts access to London's most desirable venues, hotels, security, luxury travel and private jets. I wanted to offer a concierge service in London that couldn't be matched anywhere else. I understood that Mr G was interested in possibly becoming involved at some level, as he knew London like the back of his hand and was well connected. I couldn't get his contacts and he definitely couldn't get mine, but if we could put them together we would have a great client base. With this in mind, we agreed Mr G would work from this new office and contribute to the rent. He also worked out of an office in Canary Wharf but this Mayfair office was a better location for him when he was in the West End.

I still needed to find somewhere for me and Emma to live so I called an old pal of mine who owned some property in London. He said he had a flat in Belgravia I could rent for 12 months and it would be available in a few weeks' time. It was within walking distance of my new office and the nightclub, so it was perfect. A matter of days before we were due to move in, he pulled out of the deal as he'd sold the flat. It was a real nuisance because Emma had just bought two French bulldog puppies from Harrods so we extended our stay at the Mayfair Hotel. Although initially they weren't too keen on the puppies staying, the staff were extremely accommodating and even set up a play area for them in our room. The extra time at the Mayfair Hotel actually worked out quite well as I formed a good relationship with the manager there and the hotel became a good contact for Huxley of London.

I was pissed off with my pal for backtracking on our agreement at the last minute, but he put me in touch with an estate agent called Diane who said she could find me a similar property in that area. Within a couple of days she found me another flat on Eaton Place in Belgravia. My new neighbours were Joan Collins and Maggie Thatcher! I couldn't believe how tight the security was, but I suppose it made sense as it was very close to Buckingham Palace and several foreign embassies.

Over the next month I spent a great deal of time with Mr G, familiarising myself with London and other rival nightclubs. Naturally Emma was pissed off as I hardly saw her but I was completely focussed on carrying out my competitor research properly. I didn't know London well at all, but Mr G seemed to have his finger on the pulse. By the second month we were becoming quite good pals and I'd introduced him to some of my close football friends. Mr G had also invited me and Emma to his lovely big home in Essex to meet his family. The more time I spent with Mr G and got to know him, the more I gathered that he had his fingers in several pies.

***

My life in London was busy, challenging and hard work. This was a different kind of work to what I'd been used to previously. The days were longer and less structured but I was enjoying the change of direction. I was busy with preparations at the club, piles of paperwork and getting the concierge business up and running. I'd taken on a lot in a short space of time and had my hands full; nevertheless, I was always open to new ideas and other businesses I could become involved in. An acquaintance of mine worked in the security industry and introduced me to a company based in Hereford that specialised in manufacturing military equipment for the Ministry of Defence. The company was made up of ex-special forces soldiers who were looking for investment for a product they had been developing – an unhackable, secure mobile phone. I was very interested. I love these kinds of gadgets. It was a hot topic in the media as the News of the World hacking scandal had just been exposed. I met them to test out the product but there was a delay between speaking on the phone and the other person hearing you. It still needed work, but in theory the idea was good and I realised there was definitely a market for this type of gadget. I knew a lot of people who would want one of these phones. High-ranking government officials use these types of phones already, but being able to release something like this to a mass market had huge potential. However, the final prototype just wasn't up to scratch and I pulled out of the deal at the last minute. I was disappointed as I thought it could have been very lucrative, but it was too great a risk.

26
Deception

Mr G thought it would be a good idea to check out the nightclub VIP Rooms in Paris, an exclusive venue owned by one of his contacts Jean-Roch. We drove over to the French capital and checked into a hotel. When we pulled up at the club I was amazed at how beautiful the building was; it was clear that no expense had been spared on the interiors. It had a restaurant that overlooked a rotating dance floor and the light shows were incredible. The experience was mind-blowing. We had an unbelievable night and in my opinion it was probably one of the best clubs I'd seen in Europe. Nothing I'd been to in London could compare with this, and I could understand why the VIP Rooms brand had been a global success. It gave me some great ideas to experiment with for the club on Dean Street.

During the journey back, Mr G mentioned a second nightclub opportunity on Margaret Street, just off Regent Street that I might be interested in. For the right price, he said he could get me the licence for the nightclub formerly known as Cameo, and that there weren't many central London nightclubs that operate with a licence until 7am. Immediately I thought the Dean Street club could act as a feeder to the Margaret Street one. Mr G told me that

Jean-Roch might want to rent the venue and bring the VIP Rooms brand to London. If this idea came off it would be a great business move for me! The VIP Rooms brand has an incredible international following, so if there was the slightest possibility that it might come to London, I wanted to get in there first. But even if he didn't want to rent the club, having a nightclub in central London with a 7am licence was a very attractive opportunity.

Not long after our Paris trip, Mr G invited me to a lunch at the Mayfair Hotel with Jean-Roch, Simon Webbe (from the boy band Blue) and Rick Yune (the Hollywood actor from 'The Fast and the Furious'). I remember having lunch thinking what a surreal mix of people to be sat with! There was Simon who had sold millions of records during his boy band days; Jean was one of the biggest nightclub owners in the world and he collaborated with top artists; Rick was a Hollywood star who was about to shoot with Russell Crowe in his next movie. There was me who used to kick a little white ball around, and then there was Mr G who… well, I don't really know what he actually did apart from put people around a table.

That weekend I paid him to obtain the licence and trusted him to deliver as he had done when we completed on the Dean Street club.

**

I was surprised I didn't miss playing football more than I did, especially considering just how much of my life had been about the game, but the buzz I felt on acquiring my first nightclub was immense. There was a lot to think about and masses of details to go over which kept me extremely busy.

Due to the Dean Street club being stripped out in preparation for its renovations, I spent most of my time in the Mayfair office setting up the concierge business. When football players were visiting London they would call the office to organise their stay at the best hotels, top restaurants and the most exclusive clubs. Huxley of London had made good progress in a short space of time and I'd managed to make some very useful contacts in the 'right' places. Footballers love to wind down and party after a game, and eventually my ultimate goal would be to take them to the Dean Street club for a night out rather than sending them to a rival venue.

I would pop my head into the club every day to check on its progress. A few months into the stripping-out process, I picked up the post on my way back to the office. It was usually just junk which I binned, but as I sorted through it I was astonished to find letters from debt collection agencies and bailiffs, demanding money for unpaid bills. The figures amassed to tens of thousands of pounds! As far as I was concerned the club wasn't in the red at all, so to have received all of these unpaid bills was an absolute fucking piss-take.

After several heated and frustrating phone calls to the relevant companies, I managed to figure out that these outstanding invoices were dated prior to my involvement in the business.

Once I was clearer about the situation, rather than feeling confused, my bewilderment gradually turned to anger and I called my accountant immediately. How could we not have known about this? The accountant seemed to be just as shocked as I was and said from a legal perspective I had two choices. I was now liable to pay 50% of all these outstanding debts irrespective of whether I was involved in the company or not when they were accumulated. The other option would be to go to court as he felt we could prove strongly that these debts had not been declared during the due diligence process, but I would have to halt the refurbishment and start legal action straight away. The problem with this option was that there was no guarantee I would be able to recoup any funds. I came off the phone seething and I wondered if Mr G had had some knowledge of the company's true financial position before I became involved.

To establish the nightclub's accurate debt there was a lot of paperwork to be done and phone calls to be made. I decided to bring in two bright young lads, Mike and Sam, who'd been well educated at Sedburgh School in Cumbria, to help unravel the mess in front of me. I'd known Mike's father for many years and had become quite close with his family. It was agreed that the lads would work from the Mayfair office to help me compile a file of all the outstanding debt owed by the nightclub that I was unaware of to date.

Shortly after Mike and Sam began working in the

office, Mr G stopped coming in, which I found strange as he would usually appear most days. And when I tried to call him, he didn't answer his phone. Bearing in mind the amount of time we'd been spending together, I felt a bit put out. It was odd. But I knew something was seriously wrong when the quarterly rent was due to be paid on the nightclub and Mr G's associates failed to produce their half. Alarm bells were now ringing about the huge sum of money I'd paid him for the second nightclub on Margaret Street.

I frantically tried to get hold of him but he wouldn't take my calls; nor was he available at his Canary Wharf office when I attempted to contact him there. I then received a tip-off from the architect Adrian that he was about to meet Mr G at the club himself. He was pissed off at Mr G about some work he'd completed but hadn't been paid for. The timing was perfect. Together with Mike and Sam, we'd just finished compiling a file of evidence, so now I had everything I needed to sit down with the shareholders and remove them. But I wanted to be there myself to see Mr G's eyes.

Knowing the exact time of Adrian and Mr G's meeting I went down to the club before them to wait in one of the side rooms. When they finally arrived I came up behind Mr G and thanked Adrian for his call. I asked him to leave the building.

The look on Mr G's face was a picture. Adrian was already halfway up the stairs towards the exit when Mr G started shouting for him to come back. I told Adrian to

fuck off out of the building and that he had no business
here. He didn't need to be told twice. I probably shouldn't
have shouted at Adrian. It wasn't necessary. He'd done
me a favour telling me about this meeting. However, his
association with Mr G and the whole messy situation had
got me wound up.

I tore into Mr G and demanded the money back
in full that I'd paid him for the Margaret Street club. He
agreed to repay me within seven days. I told him I wanted
nothing further to do with him or his associates. Mr G
assured me that he would ensure they removed themselves
as shareholders. I left the building to go back to the office,
and turned my attention to setting up an urgent meeting
with the shareholders. I made sure the accountant and a
solicitor were present to witness the discussions. I also
felt it was appropriate for all the other relevant people
to be there, including Clive Platt the footballer who had
recommended Mr G and his associates in the first place.

The objective of the meeting was to gain 100%
shareholding of the Dean Street nightclub. I also wanted
everyone involved to see the amount of hidden debt
there was and the true position of the company prior to
my involvement. They already knew I'd given Mr G more
money for another club on Margaret Street but I told them
he'd agreed to pay me back the following week.

Mr G's associate couldn't wait to sign over his 42.5%
shareholding. He looked ashamed and embarrassed. A
deal was then negotiated with the other shareholder and
he also signed over his 7.5%.

Once the paperwork was taken care of, I requested that both the accountant and the solicitor leave the room. I asked Clive Platt in front of everyone else if he'd known that any of this was going on, as he'd been the one to bring these people to the table. Clive Platt swore blind he knew nothing about it and I believed him.

Everyone eventually left the boardroom but I stayed. I was relieved to have removed these people from the business, but I knew I was standing at the bottom of a very steep mountain. I now owned 100% of the nightclub but this meant I also had to pay all the debts, the rent and the refurbishment costs. The clock was ticking. I had less than four years left on the current lease and the club was still in the process of being stripped out.

A week later I received a call from Mr G. He told me he was bringing the money in full that night and would meet me at 10pm on Berkeley Square. I found it unusual that he wanted to meet that late at night with so much cash on him. I didn't feel comfortable with the situation. I might have been naïve about the business world, but I knew how to look after myself. I felt like it was a set-up, so I decided to put a few lads in place to monitor the meeting as a vast amount of money could be exchanging hands.

I arrived 30 minutes before the designated time. The square was still bustling with people as the London Art Fair was on. I sat in my car waiting, constantly checking the time. Deep down I'd already realised he wasn't coming but I held out, hoping he might prove me wrong. When it got to 11pm I had to face facts. He wasn't ever going to show up with the money.

I spent months and months chasing the little cunt, trying to get him to pay up. In the end, I had no choice but to write off the money.

∗∗∗

There are no words to describe how I felt. I'd never experienced that level of anger and hatred before. I had some dark, vengeful thoughts in my head but I sensibly chose not to act on them because no amount of money is worth going to prison over. I was embarrassed that I'd been ripped off and had lost so much money. As I replayed the last few months over in my head and the people Mr G had introduced me to along the way, it became apparent that he'd just put well-known people* around the table to gain the credibility he needed to entice me to hand over more money. I'd spent pretty much every day with him. He'd welcomed me into his family home and I'd met those closest to him. He'd come through a reputable source, for fuck's sake – another footballer I trusted. So I'd had no reason to doubt anything he said. I thought we were mates and so now I was furious with him, but I was also bitterly disappointed in myself for not seeing him for the snake he was. All I could do was pick myself up and get on with the task ahead of me. I'd taken a severe blow but now I would focus solely on the club.

*I would like to make it absolutely clear that Simon Webbe, Jean-Roch and Rick Yune had nothing to do with Mr G ripping me off.

27
79 Oxford Street

With so much going on, I'd neglected my relationship with Emma. Yet again I'd made the mistake of concentrating too much on my career and on what I wanted. She was a lovely girl but things weren't right for us. She packed her stuff and took the dogs up to her mum's. In order to be truly happy you both have to fully commit to each other, and no matter how tough things get you should always give the person you love most in the world at that time your full attention and support. I couldn't give Emma that. I'd taken on a hell of a lot, probably too much, leaving me with very little free time to do anything else. A small part of me will always regret not having given her the attention she deserved.

I met with a mate of mine in Mayfair to discuss my financial position. We talked in detail about all of my outstanding personal loans to some of my football friends, my shareholding in the nightclub, the current situation there, in particular the refurbishment costs, the debt, and the fact that Mr G still hadn't repaid the money that related to the Margaret Street club. I'd lost a lot of money and it had hit me hard. After our discussion, my mate agreed to lend me £2 million and an agreement was drawn up on 11th November 2011 through our solicitors. Both parties were happy to sign it. I felt I could start to turn these circumstances around if I could just finish the club and open its doors. But in January 2012, the Daily Mail wrote two articles accusing me of being linked to a Ponzi scheme and they mentioned the concierge business. The article was rubbish and totally untrue.

The negative media had a hugely detrimental effect, crippling Huxley of London. Most high-profile people don't want to be associated with that kind of media attention and the phones simply stopped ringing. My contacts in London also dried up. I was furious about the content of the article and I spoke to a legal firm about taking action against the Daily Mail, but due to my financial position I couldn't afford to take them on in court. It was another blow that worsened an already tough time. I dusted myself off and focussed on what was important, finishing the nightclub. It was all I could do. I couldn't let my frustration or anger cloud what I was trying to achieve.

By now I'd managed to pay all the outstanding debts on the club and the company was out of the red. Annoyingly, Westminster Council knocked an hour off the licence, thanks to the trouble the previous owners had had when it was known as Maya. I called everyone I owed personal loans to and let them know they would have to wait a while until I was back on my feet. They were very understanding. They trusted me completely because I'd never let them down before. They knew what my work ethic was like and understood I would be working as hard as I possibly could to get the club finished and open. Many of them would pop by when they were in London to see how it was coming along. The doors were always open and I was there seven days a week.

I'd had some experience in renovating residential properties but not commercial ones, so nothing could have prepared me for the myriad of issues we faced. Anyone who has completed a major refurbishment knows how much commitment and effort it takes to see it through. And doing this in central London takes renovating to a whole new level of complicated. I had a mammoth team of people on the project. There were always people coming and going, and someone was there 24/7. Due to its prime Soho location we couldn't have a skip on-site or outside. We had to organise vans to arrive at 3am every morning to take all the waste away.

The area already had its fair share of late-night bars so we had to deal with people urinating on the front door and homeless people setting up camp on the doorstep. There was very little parking so most of the builders ended up sleeping in the club throughout the week. I'd spend hours down in the basement mucking in with the lads. Those early days I'd spent working with my uncle definitely came in useful! There wasn't any natural light down there so when anyone came up for air, it took a while for your eyes to adjust to the daylight. It was organised chaos – a hive of noise with a constant smell of freshly sawn wood.

Despite the stress and the endless dust, I was thoroughly enjoying it. I was learning a hell of a lot on the job. I thrived on the logistical problem-solving. I loved working with all the different tradesmen and picking up new basic skills. I was very 'hands on' and wanted to be as much a part of building the club as I was designing it.

The club had been through so many refurbishments over the years and as a result the space inside was much smaller than what was portrayed in the floor plans. I wanted to completely open it up and return it to an empty shell; my vision was to allow people in the club to experience light shows and performances, but this required more space. However, while the builders were busy working on stripping the floor, they had to stop because there was suspected asbestos. The basement was evacuated and I called in the HSE people. They closed the area off for a month and no one was allowed on-site except for a specialised asbestos company who came to remove it. Once it was safe, we continued with the refit but the hours we could work were restricted by Pizza Hut who were situated directly above us, as they couldn't have us beavering away below them with noisy kango drills.

After the entire basement had been stripped out I finally felt we were making progress, but the reality was I'd just opened up Pandora's box. We realised there was a lot of water coming in from the pavement above, along Oxford Street and Dean Street. I had to call in another specialist company to honeycomb damp-proof the affected parts of the ceilings and walls, then drill out sumps in the concrete floor to allow the excess water to flow into the drainage system. It seemed that nothing was a simple task.

Cross Rail, as part of a £14.8 billion project, were

also in the process of tunnelling a railway line beneath us with their giant machinery. I was slightly concerned when one of the site managers came to ask if they could install some water vibration monitors throughout the club. They wanted to observe the movement of the structural pillars.

It was around this time that I decided to bring in my old mucker Jude Stirling. He was coming to the end of his footballing career and he'd had a few injuries, which were starting to take their toll. I could see he needed a fresh challenge. I also needed the help. Like most footballers who start their careers at a young age, he didn't plan too far ahead. Many find that when it comes to hanging up their boots, there's never a great deal of opportunity. I knew Jude had fuck-all experience in commercial building work or running a nightclub but we'd been friends for 15 years so I knew he was trustworthy, loyal and a grafter. After what had happened with Mr G and the other shareholders, I felt he was the major component I needed.

There were now less than three years left on the current lease. The plan was to complete the basement with a high-spec finish to not only attract the kind of clients I was aiming for, but also to impress the landlord so we could negotiate a new lease.

I wanted to create a concept that matched what people remember on a fantastic night out. We came up with the brand name Stamp, which stood for Service, Technology and Music Performance. I loved what the graphic designers had done with the logo. We used bright, vivid colours and carried out a lot of research on profiling to understand the club's target demographic. We crafted a brand image that was exactly what I'd envisaged when I initially bought into the club. In spite of the previous pitfalls, I believed things were looking up and we were making good progress. It was slow and desperately painful at times but most importantly we were moving in the right direction.

The company's licensing solicitor had been working vigorously with Westminster Council and the Metropolitan Police. We were constantly in discussion with them, aiming to prove that what we were trying to build was the polar opposite of what the previous venue, Maya, had been. I knew that if we could convince them, the council and the police would be more lenient regarding the current licence's restrictions.

Once the club had been stripped back to its core, the space was great. One of the fire-exit doors at the back of the club opened up onto Oxford Street. I remember wondering why this door had never been used as a main entrance. After looking at the plans, I realised this wasn't part of our lease; it was a void space between the nightclub and Pizza Hut.

I called the landlord to find out more about the situation. He said he was in a position to lease that part of the basement to the company and would come down to see me. When that time came, we talked about my plans for making it the main entrance. Apart from the old 100 Club, I didn't believe any other venue had its main entrance on Oxford Street itself. It would provide us with a grander, more attractive entrance and a more recognisable address: 79 Oxford Street.

We negotiated and he said he was happy to give us a very cheap rental rate. It was great news and I accepted it straight away, informing him that the company solicitor would be in touch immediately. I wasn't really listening properly to what he went on to say, as in my head I was excitedly running through all the design possibilities for the new main entrance. During the conversation, I thought I heard him say, "*demolish the building*."

I came crashing down to reality very rapidly. Had I heard him correctly? I asked him to repeat what he'd just said.

"The entire building is to be demolished in 2015."

I looked at him blankly. I even think I laughed in his face through sheer shock. I thought he was joking. What he'd just repeated sounded ludicrous, but the word "*demolished*" kept ringing in my ears. I couldn't work out what was happening. I'd spoken to his colleague numerous times and nothing had ever been mentioned about the building being knocked down. I had no idea what the fuck he was talking about.

Noticing that my face had turned a dull shade of green, he explained that the previous owners had been well aware that the leases were not to be renewed due to the building's planned demolition. He thought I knew. The east end of Oxford Street was being regenerated and this building formed part of the multi-million pound redevelopment. He even said he wondered why we'd been doing so much work down here. I just stared at him. Gaping. After what felt like an eternity of dumbfounded silence, I regained some semblance of composure and started firing questions at him.

"Do you have a fixed demolition date?"

"Is there any way to extend the lease?"

"Is this definitely going to happen?"

I was dazed. I felt like someone had punched me in the face and knocked me out. I'd bought into this project thinking I'd be able to negotiate a further 10-20 years on the lease. He said the most they might be able to do was give the company an extra six months but he would have to let me know. I thanked him for his time but was left standing there feeling totally numb – feeling like the ground had opened beneath me and swallowed me up. Based on projected forecasts the company had just lost a potential £10 million.

I thought we would have been in that one location for years to come; that Stamp would become synonymous with 79 Oxford Street. The time, effort and money that had already been poured into the project left me feeling sick to my stomach. I realised then that Mr G had targeted me. He was the one who'd approached me to construct the deal in the first place despite already knowing, in my opinion, about the company's debts and that the lease would never be renewed. I'd even used a solicitor he'd recommended. He'd lined me up good and proper.

I'm a pretty measured character and my life's experiences have hardened me. I'm Scottish so I'm naturally passionate, but I'm not exactly what you'd call emotional and I always tend to take a pragmatic approach to life. But that day I honestly thought my head was going to explode.

This had gone from being an exciting project to a noose around my neck. Jude and I had sacrificed a lot. I'd barely seen the light of day. He'd barely seen his kids, because most nights we slept and ate there. My life had drastically changed, going from training and working half-days to 24-hour shifts in a dungeon. I'd stopped socialising as I thought it was a piss-take to be seen out and about when there was so much to do. Now I had to try to recoup some of the money I'd borrowed. I believed in our concept but I would never have invested so much time and detailed planning into the design if I'd known the lease was going to be so short. I would just have given it a lick of paint and worked on pulling in some new clients!

I didn't know what to think or what to do with myself, but dwelling on it would drive me mad and it certainly wouldn't help me finish what I'd started. Right now I had to make the best of what I had in front of me and not let it hold me back. Even if all I could have was a few months' extension it was better than nothing as I could trade for a year or so and at least promote the brand. A short successful run might give me the opportunity to move to another venue. I was now in a huge hurry to finish the refurbishment and with funds running low, I decided to sell shares in the business to help complete the project.

When it came to new shareholders I couldn't be

overly fussy about who came on board. Some were people I knew personally but others came through third-party recommendations which wasn't ideal but that was the situation I was in. What was encouraging, though, was that certain people to whom I already owed personal loans wanted to become involved with the company to help me cross the finishing line – even after I'd made them aware of the lease situation. Jude and I were always mindful of retaining full control of the company so that we could ensure the concept was delivered exactly as we envisioned it.

28
Grass Roots

Jude's father, Clasford Stirling, is a legend in North London and is heavily involved in the Broadwater Farm Community Centre. For his efforts, in 2007 he was awarded an MBE for Services to Sport because across the community Clasford did and still does an unbelievable job in bringing everyone together. He has mentored hundreds of young footballers including his son Jude, Emmanuel Frimpong and Jobi McAnuff.

Jude suggested it might be a good idea to set up a non-league football team and give something back to the game we both loved. In the short term Broadwater United would act as a type of feeder club to the team and in return give young kids the chance to play alongside experienced ex-professionals. It would be a welcome distraction for us both to get out of the nightclub and breathe in some fresh air. I hadn't played football since my Coventry City days and I was keen to put a pair of football boots on again.

We asked Clasford to manage the team, while Jude and I would try our best to coach the kids as we played alongside them. It made me think about the coaching I'd received from the senior pros during my early days as a young professional at Luton Town FC. I loved the idea of being able to pass on some of my own footballing knowledge and teach some aspiring young footballers what I wish I'd known at their age.

Although the nightclub took priority, Jude and I tried to fit in as many games as we could for our team London Elite FC. It was great to be kicking a ball around again and it gave me a taste of that familiar buzz I used to get. It felt natural to have a ball back at my feet. I hadn't realised how much I'd missed it.

Hertford Town FC were kind enough to let us share their stadium for our home matches and to give us our first ever game, where they beat us 2-0. Despite losing, the talent Clasford had extracted from Broadwater Farm surpassed my expectations. Yes, they needed some work but the amount of raw talent within the team was superb and gave us an excellent foundation to start from. I decided they were probably ready for some tougher matches so we went to Telford United in the Conference and Oldham Athletic in League One. Although we were just outside the FA footballing structure, I wanted the kids to play against higher-division opposition to show them what the standard was really like outside the Premier League. It would be invaluable experience for them.

Telford United only beat us 1-0. We out-passed them for most of the first half. There was no doubt in my mind that some of these kids were ready to go straight into the professional game. It's a shame that professional teams located near Broadwater Farm don't look closer to home when they're seeking new talent.

Our next match was against Oldham Athletic.

My former teammate Lee Johnson had recently been appointed to the managerial post. The League One season was a week away from starting and he'd promised to field a strong team. Before kick-off I warned the kids that the Oldham lads would be going for the jugular that day. I knew Lee would definitely want to win. Call it friendly rivalry between former teammates! When we arrived at the ground, I could see the excitement in the kids' eyes. This was a unique experience for them. It was an extraordinary feeling being able to give these kids such an opportunity.

After 20 minutes we were losing 2-1; the kids tried their best to keep the score down but eventually the gulf between the teams started to show and the floodgates opened. I lost count after six goals. When the game finished the kids sat in the changing room, thoroughly deflated. The biggest lessons they'd learnt were how fit the other players were and how fast the tempo of the game was. I reassured them that there was no shame in that defeat; the exercise had simply been to demonstrate how much hard work they would need to put in, if their true aspiration was to play in the professional game.

.

29
The Grand Opening

After two and a half years our persistence had paid off and we finally finished the club. The Oxford Street entrance had been approved, so the club could now open its doors onto one of Europe's busiest streets. Jude and I had managed to keep a controlling stake in the business and now the company had around 20 shareholders along with some big international sponsors. Without them there's no way the venue could have been completed.

Yes, it had taken more than double the amount of time and a hell of a lot more money and effort than originally anticipated, but this was my first commercial renovation project and the feeling of achievement I experienced was overwhelming. The venue was fully stocked and ready to go. It looked incredible. The large main entrance was a replica of a shiny, steel vault door, with a polish-plastered corridor that led down to the basement level. From here, sound-proofed, velvet double doors opened into the main room, where a two-tiered seating area surrounded two elevated stages. These platforms would be the focal point for artists' performances.

An electronic track system was fixed to the ceiling to fly small people through the air, creating a highly theatrical effect. The entire club was fitted with an exceptional light and sound system; even the drinks tables lit up to the beat of the music. Our sound-engineering room had more gadgets than the inside of a spaceship, so we brought in Jude's brother Daniel who's a very talented music producer to help set up all the gizmos to create spectacular light and sound shows. Jude and I had already agreed that the company could reuse the newly installed sound system and equipment in another venue. We took care to ensure that such items would be easy to access and remove without damaging. In fact, most of the final fit-out could be removed and used again elsewhere.

I believed in the brand and wanted to give it a real go. The opening night took place on 14th February 2014 and the venue was three-quarters full, which wasn't bad considering there had been very little marketing in the run-up to the event. The security staff had refused entry to quite a few people so we definitely could have packed the place out, but I wanted to adhere to our strict members-only policy and attract the right kind of clientele. We had a few teething problems, which was to be expected, but overall I felt it was a reasonable start.

Having never managed a nightclub before, it took a few nights to get into the flow of it. I wanted to run a tight ship with a military-style level of efficiency. The 26 tables had been split into sections with a Vice President taking charge of a particular area. It was the VP's job to bring in big spenders. They had to be out and about in top London bars and restaurants before the club opened, rounding up the best clients; the bigger the spend the bigger their commission. They each had a team of butlers who would take drinks orders and ensure that tables were replenished throughout the evening. I expected everyone, except the VPs, to be at the club by 9pm ready to rock and roll at 10pm when the doors opened.

The venue operated mainly by table service, and the club's menu offered shows ranging from around £5,000 to £50,000, whereby our members would have the opportunity to buy a mini theatre performance along with champagne. For most people this sounds crazy but for a group of eight people or more at this sort of venue, it's pretty standard to spend in excess of £5,000. The clients you really want are the ones who spend £20,000 and above in a single night. In London there are a handful of clubs that can turn over £100,000-£150,000 per week. One of the other reasons I wanted to own nightclubs in central London was because of the markup on alcohol. Single bottles could achieve a markup of up to 500% and some limited-edition bottles can be sold for tens of thousands of pounds.

During the first month of trading, the Metropolitan Police and the Westminster licensing officer visited every other night. I used to watch them arrive on the CCTV; the club's ex-military police security team, wearing military-style uniforms, would welcome them and escort them down to my office. As the new proprietor, I would sit with them for 20 minutes during the club's peak time to ensure I was adhering to the strict licensing regulations. It was a pain in the arse. However, with hundreds of people in the venue at any one time, some of them high net worth, and the occasional foreign royal, we could have been a target for an act of terrorism. I think they were impressed and could see we hadn't cut any corners. We had certainly been thorough.

Following the first month of trading I was able to get a clearer picture of the financial situation. I was new to this, but it didn't take a genius to work out that the club was paying out a lot more than it was bringing in – with the biggest expense being the staff. I was overpaying some of them. I knew I needed to restructure. It had been a slower start than expected but I believe this was due to an initial lack of marketing. Now it was open and word was slowly spreading, it was only a matter of time before business picked up. Obviously the shareholders wanted a return on their investment, and a few sub-contractors were still waiting to receive their final payment. I realised that by letting a few of the staff go and reducing wages, I would decrease the overheads by at least 30%. I could then start to balance the books before making a profit.

30
Timing is Everything

Jude told me there were a few whispers being passed between the shareholders about our lack of profit in the first month, but the reality was we'd only just started trading and as with any business it would take time to grow. I think because the concept was so good everybody thought, including me, that from day one it would go off with a bang. In fact, I'd been so busy with everything else I hadn't put enough time into marketing the club, which was a big mistake. However, I just hadn't had the time and I'd left it to the people I'd hired to deliver what they said they could.

I decided to speak to a few of the shareholders to ask them to be patient. We'd only been trading for a month. Over the course of the renovation process we'd used a hell of a lot of different sub-contractors. The majority had all been paid in full but there were a small handful who hadn't received their final payment yet. I'd personally contacted those who remained and explained that as soon as the club started making a profit they would receive their payment. All of them had informed me that they were happy to wait as they'd already received a large percentage of their total invoice. So I was astonished to learn that the design company I'd used had served a petition to wind up the nightclub on 12th March 2014. Legally, the person concerned was well within her rights to start legal action. Her company had already been paid approximately 60% of the invoice, but unfortunately at that time the nightclub wasn't in a position to pay the final amount. I'd hit another brick wall.

The thing that baffled me the most, though, was that this sub-contractor was actually the ex-wife of the mate I'd previously signed a loan agreement with for £2 million! I couldn't understand why she would want to wind up a business that was my only possible source of income, in order to pay back her ex-husband. The two of them had remained close and saw each other most days so it wasn't as if they had a terrible relationship and she wanted him to suffer. They were extremely amicable. He hadn't mentioned anything to me about it either. Surely he must have been aware? They both knew how hard I'd worked on this project over the last few years. Given what had happened to me with Mr G, I'd developed a much more suspicious mindset and I found it hard to believe that the timing of this winding-up petition wasn't just a coincidence. But maybe that was the whole point?

I spoke to the company's solicitor and the accountant to find out what the club's options were in this kind of situation. Then I had a meeting with one of the shareholders, and he informed me that if I were to resign as director, he would settle any of the club's outstanding bills. I didn't know what to do. I had a few sleepless nights; I was in a tough place. I'd invested nearly three years of my life in this project. It had consumed me. The energy and effort that had gone into it were immense. So the thought of resigning sickened me, yet I felt I'd taken the company as far as I could. I was bitterly disappointed but I just couldn't see any other option. I definitely wasn't going to let the club go under after everything I'd endured. This way, the club could stay open, the staff could retain their jobs and the sub-contractors could receive their final payments. These, for me, were the most important aspects.

After a long discussion with Jude and much deliberation, I resigned as director on 30th April 2014.

With very little left to stay in London for, I travelled to Scotland to clear my head. Jude came with me and we jumped on a train to Fort William in the Highlands to climb Ben Nevis, a favourite pastime of mine. I'd been before and always enjoyed returning to go camping. The dramatic backdrop of the Highlands is probably one of the most beautiful views in the world. The vast, rugged wilderness offers a serenity that only my home country can give me. I love the trek up Ben Nevis; it's a brutal climb but about three-quarters of the way up the mountain there's a particular spot where I always like to stop to inhale the fresh clean air, take in the scenery and drink the clear water running down from the summit.

Being in a relaxed state of mind, free from electronics and the distractions of everyday life, offers me the breathing space to think calmly. Jude and I talked a lot but I also did a great deal of thinking while we were up there. Since leaving football almost three years previously,

I hadn't taken a break to allow myself time to reflect and unwind. Instead, I'd thrown myself into the hectic business life of London. I had desperately wanted the nightclub to be a success but unfortunately this wasn't to be.

Jude travelled back to London but I stopped off in Edinburgh to see some old friends and family. I hadn't seen my mother for ages and thought it best to pop my head in while I was up there. Over the years my mother's mental health has slowly deteriorated, but she still has that famous Scottish fire in her belly. And although she smokes 30 fags a day, she'll probably live until she's 110. I know that moving away from Scotland at an early age had huge benefits for me, but I also sacrificed some good friendships and family ties that I will never retrieve. I'd had to be incredibly selfish to achieve my own dreams, so it was good to finally have the time to see many familiar faces. It was just what I needed.

31
Black Hole

On 31st October 2014, my debit card was declined while trying to withdraw money from a cashpoint. I'd only just used it so I made that annoying phone call to my bank to find out why my card wasn't working. The call handler told me my account was frozen due to bankruptcy. I quizzed her, asking for more details, but she was quite vague and passed me on to another department, which then put me on hold and passed me on again. I was pissed off at being passed around and just wanted some answers. After explaining myself to several different call handlers, I was eventually given a name and number to contact.

The next person I spoke to was a Trustee in Bankruptcy. He told me that my so-called 'mate' who I'd signed the loan agreements with had served a bankruptcy petition to the High Court in London a few months earlier in July 2014 for an amount of around £3 million. I was then declared bankrupt on 14th October 2014. I realised the paperwork had been served to an incorrect address; hence I'd known nothing of the bankruptcy. Believe it or not, you can be declared bankrupt without knowing anything about it.

The Trustee then explained to me that his role was to sell my assets in order to make payments to creditors during the bankruptcy period of 12 months. The Trustee also worked in conjunction with an Official Receiver whose role was to oversee each bankruptcy case.

This was also the same 'mate' whose ex-wife had served a winding-up petition on the nightclub. After I'd got over the initial shock, I contacted him. He agreed to meet me a quarter of a mile from his house. I wanted to ask him what he was doing? I wanted to ask him if he'd really thought this through? He was aware of my financial position and he knew my assets wouldn't cover the outstanding amount owed, so he was essentially writing off a large part of the debt. Perhaps he could afford to write it off? I didn't know.

When we met, there was an altercation. He went straight to the police and the next thing I knew Doncaster CID were interviewing me regarding an allegation of GBH. I was bailed for a few months pending a forensic report. No charges were ever brought against me.

My 'mate' who lent me the £2 million, whose ex-wife tried to wind up the nightclub, who made the allegation of GBH to the police, and who filed the petition for my bankruptcy is Michael Patrick Murray – also known as Mick Murray from Doncaster. I'd known Mick and his family for over ten years. I originally met him through my ex-girlfriend Helen during my Doncaster Rovers' days. It's his son Mike who helped me to identify the unforeseen debt when I first became involved in the nightclub and who's dating Mike Ashley's daughter Anna.

I'd like to say that at the time I was overwhelmed

with a mixture of emotions, but I wasn't. Even though the bankruptcy should have engulfed me in a whole new level of stress, I remained quite calm. I'd taken several knocks in the last few years and I'd grown up in a pretty destitute environment, so I wasn't completely thrown by this. Plus, I had some unbelievably strong people around me who, luckily for me, were willing to help me out.

I didn't really understand what was involved but after some research I realised that bankruptcy is far more common than I'd originally thought. According to The Money Charity's UK debt statistics, over 200 people a day are declared insolvent or bankrupt. This is equivalent to one person every six minutes. I had no idea it was as common as this. The word bankrupt and the people who fall into the black hole of bankruptcy have always attracted a certain stigma in society, so initially I was quite concerned about what this all meant and how it would impact on my life. It wasn't actually as bad as I first thought it would be. My solicitor asked me not to contact anyone, to help where I could, and to leave the bankruptcy process to run its course. Which is what I've done.

Then I was introduced to ES Life Coaching through a friend. Having worked successfully with psychologists in the past, I wondered whether working in a less intense way with a life coach might help me to refocus on my future personal goals and get me through this next chapter of my life. I decided to take part in some sessions in London and I worked on putting a new ten-year plan in place, breaking it down into smaller segments to make it more achievable.

The sessions helped me to recognise that although this wasn't an ideal situation, if there was ever a time for this to happen now was probably the best because I didn't have kids who relied on me to put a roof over their heads. I can imagine that if I'd had those kinds of responsibilities I would have found it much more stressful and harder to deal with. Maybe this was why I was so unruffled by it all.

I travelled up and down the country to attend interviews and cross-examinations under oath in the High Court on several occasions, most of which were standard protocol. It's not a particularly pleasant process to undergo, and I was grateful to find out that my bankrupt status would last for only 12 months. I lost property as well as my bank account. Some might see that as the end of the world but at 35 years of age I still had plenty of time to have another go at life.

Another positive was that I'd reached a 15-year milestone of not drinking – something only a handful of people will understand but for me this was a huge personal achievement. It made me remember that I had endured much worse and I still had a lot to be thankful for. Rather than dwell on the negatives, I prefer to search for the positives in every situation.

During my 12-month bankruptcy period the Official Receiver who was overseeing my case applied to the High Court for a ten-year restriction order. If successful, I would have to adhere to certain restrictions for the next decade of my life. I strongly opposed her application. I felt there was no foundation whatsoever for a restriction order to be granted. I was given some time to make my case and submitted an overwhelming amount of evidence to the High Court.

It came as no surprise to me that the application was discontinued and the matter was rapidly put to bed.

***

To those people I borrowed money from but didn't pay back in full, I humbly apologise. People who know me well know that I've always been meticulous about paying back any money I've borrowed. I desperately wanted the club to be the success we all thought it would be. There were many unforeseen circumstances which I could never have planned for. I trusted certain individuals yet I should never have entertained them in the first place. I'm truly gutted things didn't work out.

32
SensationaLIESed

The most frustrating aspect of the last few years hasn't been the bankruptcy; it's been what the papers have falsely written about me. I've watched the media try to tarnish my credibility and defame my character on a monthly basis. The year I became bankrupt I received more media attention than I ever did playing football!

I've read articles which wrongly suggest that I'm the mastermind behind one of the biggest frauds to hit Britain. One paper even outrageously claimed that Chelsea legend John Terry had given me £1 million. He's never lent me a penny.

The press made it look as if I was on trial for fraud. This is not the case. I have only ever attended court due to my bankruptcy obligations.

My favourite newspaper article claimed that I was in hiding. If I were hiding, would I have turned up to every single appointment or court date that my bankruptcy required of me? I was pretty easy to track down. If anyone has ever wanted to meet with me, I've always turned up. So who the fuck am I hiding from?

In over 100 regional and national articles, the press claimed that there have been hundreds and hundreds of victims. I find it hard to believe that no one has questioned why only two sources have ever been named – one of which was the Trustee's company who made around £4 million worth of accounting errors during my bankruptcy.

False headlines such as these can destroy people's lives. I've spent the whole of my adult life trying to better myself as a person, so for my integrity to be questioned in such a way, understandably infuriates me! These articles have made it difficult for me to move forward with my life, which is why I decided I needed to provide my own account in this book, without it being twisted and manipulated just to sell papers. I didn't have the money to start legal action against big media corporations so I've had to swallow every article that has been written about me.

***

Despite all that was being alleged in the press, it might come as a surprise to many that the police never came to see me, or question me, about the false allegations the media were making against me.

I became so concerned about the seriousness of the press's accusations that I took it upon myself to personally contact the then Commissioner of the Metropolitan Police, Sir Bernard Hogan-Howe, on 18th January 2016 to find out what the hell was going on?!

A year later, on 10th January 2017, I voluntarily attended an interview with Scotland Yard in London where I made it absolutely clear that there was no wrongdoing on my part. After the interview, I was told by the DCI from Scotland Yard that they were at the end of their investigation.

I've never denied that there was money outstanding; in fact, the High Court is in receipt of documents that contain the key facts and figures.

But I will say it again – I haven't committed fraud, nor will I ever be involved in any kind of fraud.

Epilogue

Since leaving the football industry in 2011, there have been several times when I've thought about lacing up my boots again. Given everything that has happened in the last few years, it would be the obvious choice to make. I've kept myself in decent physical condition; my fitness level is probably more like that of a late 20 year-old than a 37 year-old! But the truth is, I don't believe it would be as much of a mental challenge as it once was. I still love the game, and when I watch matches I feel nostalgic, but I think the only football-related positions that would interest me now are managing or owning a football club. Yes, I still have BIG aspirations!

I might have made mistakes but I will definitely learn from them. As Bill Gates, the founder of Microsoft, once said, "It's fine to celebrate success but it is more important to heed the lessons of failure." Look, every single person will face setbacks, but it's the amount of fight and spirit you show at the time that will define you as a person. For me, whenever difficult times have occurred, my self-belief seems to have grown. This sounds strange, but after enduring some tough times and seeing them through, the experience has somehow instilled in me an inner confidence. I have an indomitable spirit and an intense, single-minded work ethic which drives me. I am a true believer in always looking forward and focussing on the positives. New doors will open for me – of that I am sure.

Index

Leyton Orient 115
Liverpool 88
Locarno Snooker Club 38
London Art Fair 213
London Elite 226
Luton Town 46-47, 53, 56, 60, 66, 68, 73, 80, 82-83, 96, 118, 133, 187, 225
Maine Road 69
Manchester City 66, 69, 125
Manchester United 129
Manchester University 90
Marbella 199-201
Marchwood Priory 9, 78
Martin (brother) 13, 32, 38-39, 68
Mayfair 202-204, 208-210, 215
Maynard, Nicky 168-169
McAnuff, Jobi 225
McCarthy, Mick 147-148, 150, 153, 161
McCoist, Ally 88, 135
McCulloch, Marc 41
McGowan, Gavin 69
McNamara, Jackie 88
McPhail, Stephen 119
McSheffrey, Gary 188
Merson, Paul 9, 80-81, 83, 92, 114, 117
Merthyr Tydfil 88, 106
Miller, Kenny 23
Millwall 136, 155
MK Dons 191
Molineux 147-148, 150, 156, 172
Moore, John 46-47, 53-57, 82-83, 145, 172, 178
Moran, Andy 88
Moxey, Jez 145, 150-151
Moyes, David 186
Moyes, Kenny 186
Mum 9, 13-14, 19, 23, 25-26, 30, 32-33, 38, 48, 74, 78, 123-124, 215
Murray, Matt 149
Musselburgh 23, 25, 39, 41, 45-46
Myhill, Boaz 165
N-Joi 31
N'Gotty, Bruno 149

Newbery, Cherry 76
Noble, David 159
Oakwell 119, 139
Old Trafford 90
Oldham Athletic 226
Orr, Bradley 164, 175
Owen, Nick 83
Owusu-Abeyie, Quincy 128
Parry, Paul 90
Peake, Trevor 56
Pearce, Stuart 125
Penney, Dave 119-121, 125, 127, 132-135, 138, 188-191
Perton 148
Peugeot 45-48
Phillips, Kevin 150
Pizza Hut 218, 220
Platt, Clive 188, 191, 199, 212-213
Plymouth 172-173
Queens Park Rangers 156
Ranson, Ray 181, 190, 193
Ratpack 31
Ravelston House Hotel 46
Real Madrid 187
Reiley, David 46
Richardson, Baz 120
Ridgewell, Liam 126
Ritchie, Andy 139, 142
Road, Gorgie 13, 37-38, 40
Roberts, Neil 129
Robinson, Phil 90
Rodgerson, Ian 87
Rooney, Wayne 123
Rotherham 115
Rushden & Diamonds 96
Ryan, John 9, 108, 110, 115, 117-119, 127, 133-134, 137, 168-169
Ryan, Phil 118
Salvesen Boys Club 23
Scotland National Team 117, 122, 131, 135, 144, 183
Sedburgh School 210
Selhurst Park 158